GESTALT AWARENESS

GESTALT AWARENESS

Papers from the San Francisco Gestalt Institute

Edited and with an Introduction by Jack Downing, M.D.

PERENNIAL LIBRARY
Harper & Row, Publishers
New York, Hagerstown, San Francisco, London

 For information address Harper & Row, Publishers, Inc., 10 East 53d Street, New York, N.Y. 10022. Published simultaneously in Canada by Fitzhenry & Whiteside Limited, Toronto.

Designed by Eve Callahan

First edition: PERENNIAL LIBRARY, 1976

LIBRARY OF CONGRESS CATALOG NUMBER: 75–27091

STANDARD BOOK NUMBER: 06–080373–8

76 77 78 79 80 10 9 8 7 6 5 4 3 2 1

Contents

Acknowledgments vii
Introduction ix

PART ONE

A Talk at the San Francisco Gestalt Institute Ram Dass 3

I. *An Encounter with Fritz Perls* 3

II. *Collecting the Questions.* Attachment and Perception; Can You Trust What I Say?; Attachment to Acts; Work on Yourself; Every Act Is a Teaching; The Therapist's Predicament; Karma and Therapy; Imposing Models; Brotherhood Is a Reality; The Sea of Ignorance; Attachment to Your Own Story Line; Free Will and Determinism; One Consciousness in All Things; Self: A Set of Processes; How Do We Learn?; Spiritual Powers; Emptying; Paradox and Dualism 5

III. *Love.* In Love; Erotic Love; Attachment to Your Guru; Nonattachment to Your Guru; The Inner Teacher; Spiritual Practices; Meditation 35

IV. *Dying.* Maharaji and Dying; Working with People Who Are Dying; Zen Monks at Mount Sinai Hospital; The Wild Strawberry Story; A Center for Dying; My Own Death 46

PART TWO

Gestalt Awareness Strategies in the Training of People–Helpers John B. Enright, Ph.D. 63

One View of Gestalt Therapy: An Evening Discussion with Trainees
Stephen Schoen, M.D. 75

Women and Gestalt Awareness Lois Brien, Ph.D., and Cynthia Sheldon, M.S.W. 91

A Gestalt Way of Using Language
Paula Bottome, Ph.D. 104

Where Do Your Lines Lead? Gestalt Art Groups Celia Thompson-Taupin, M.A.T. 112

Social Dreamwork and Gestalt Therapy
Joel Latner, Ph.D. 124

Unmasking the Face and Facing the Mask: A Gestalt Approach to Facial Therapy
Jack L. Rosenberg, Ph.D., D.D.S. 138

Acknowledgments

I want to extend my gratitude to Ivan Morvay for his assistance in writing and editing the Introduction and for his general comments as this book evolved. Also, special thanks are due to Dorothy Luttrel for her assistance in editing the talk by Ram Dass.

But most importantly, this book would not have existed without the friends and members of the San Francisco Gestalt Institute: Fritz Perls, Jim Simkin, Laura Perls, Janie Rhyne, Bob Hall, Kurt Feibush, Brian Hand, Jerry Rothstein, Art Damond, Claudio Naranjo, Dick Miller, Larry Bloomberg, Cyndy Sheldon, Abe Levistky, Lois Brien, Elaine Kepner, Stella Resnick, Paula Bottome, Celia Thompson-Taupim, Zoe Snyder, Stephen Schoen, Frank Rubenfeld, Jack Rosenberg, Joel Latner, Sid Gershenson, John Enright, Joe Camhi, Walter Barney, Jerry Kogan, Michael Conant, Ram Dass, and Jill Alexander, the administrator.

Introduction

I

Some thirty years ago, a neon sign planted on a green cottage lawn beside Wilshire Boulevard in Los Angeles blinked bluely on and off. Each bright azure flash proclaimed PSYCHOANALYSIS AND HIGH COLONIC IRRIGATION ***PSYCHOANALYSIS AND HIGH COLONIC IRRIGATION*** PSYCHOANALYSIS AND HIGH COLONIC IRRIGATION. Now Gestalt is the "in" therapy. It is our turn for the Los Angeles *Free Press*, the *Berkeley Barb*, and *Screw* to advertise boldly: GESTALT THERAPY AND SENSUAL MASSAGE and GESTALT ENCOUNTER GROUPS LED BY NUDE CUTIES.

Like our senior and venerable sibling, psychoanalysis, we are starting to become generic to the culture. Yet Gestalt is poorly understood—a fact that cannot be attributed simply to the newness and audacity of the approach, nor even to the fact that it is not yet as widely practiced as analysis. Perhaps a better reason is that Gestalt, viewed as an agreed-upon canon of theory and practice, is hard to pin down. In this, of course, it reflects the personality and mind-set of its free-flowing and unpredictable founder, Fritz Perls. He once said to me (and undoubtedly to others as well, for he richly appreciated a good line), "I'm a disappointment to those Gestalt therapists who expect me to continue doing what I've done before. They insist I'm no longer a Gestalt therapist." Possibly no operational definition of a "true" Gestalt therapist exists; certainly Fritz lived as his fancy chose, by his own enunciated precepts: live now and express now. "Eat when you're hungry, drink when you're thirsty, sleep when you're tired, screw when you're hot, and play!" That is a Zen motto, he claimed, along with another repeated favorite: "When you piss, don't smoke a cigarette." What a founder! No wonder that, to date, Gestalt has not had the ill fate to form an establishment—an academic orthodoxy to close out the marketplace and strangle its evolution—the historic fate of psychoanalysis.

Nevertheless, for all the viability that this freedom implies, the problem remains that the *process* of developing Gestalt awareness is poorly understood. We have passed the stage of explaining the content of Gestalt—there are many books on that subject. Rather, the process is what counts and it is what, hopefully, you will find writ large in this collection of papers loosely grouped about the unifying fact that they all somehow originated in connection with the San Francisco Gestalt Institute.

The attempt to pin down how the Gestalt process works will be made repeatedly in this book, both by precept and example. In keeping with my theme of linking Gestalt to what went before it, the attempt should be made in this introduction to draw at least its larger outlines. At the outset, then it seems clear that Gestalt has drawn its power from two primary sources: (1) the non-Freudians and the post-Freudians—the freethinkers, rebels and outlaws who refused to conform to the orthodox dogma of the analytic establishment, people such as Reich and Jung, Perls and Laing; (2) Eastern mysticism with its emphasis on the power of *non*doing, the futility of *trying*, and the primacy of essence over ego.

What emerges are several ways to characterize the Gestalt approach:

It is nondualistic; rather, it exposes how unconscious polarizations tie up our energies.
It is not therapy.
It is nonanalytic.
It is noninterpretive.
It denies a mind-body split.
It denies the sickness-health dichotomy.
It is not a way of life; rather, it is a way of living.

Gestalt, then, is a sort of Western Taoism—it focuses not on change but on awareness in and of itself. It focuses not on getting but on abandoning. In a paradoxical way it focuses on the power of *negative* thinking. That is, as Kenneth Burke once remarked: "yes" really means saying no to no!

All this would seem to imply that Gestalt is moving toward a concept of the self much different from that described in any of the older therapies, whether Freudian or Jungian. This movement was prefigured by Fritz Perls himself, who viewed the Gestalt process as being aimed at the self rather than at that ground of being upon which the self rests—the essence. The surface—the phenomenology of life—is all. Or as Werner Erhard puts it: "*This* is it. There are no hidden meanings. All that mystical stuff is just what's so. A master is someone who found out." It is the clarification of this vital point at which many of the papers in this book aim. The Gestalt of today thus is not, cannot be, the Gestalt of even a few years ago, and of that I am sure Fritz would approve.

Of the distinctions listed above, none is more important for the development of the Gestalt process than the two that state that it is not therapy and that it denies the sickness-health polarization. After enormous amounts of experience with the traditional therapies, it has finally become apparent that psychotherapy really effects no "cures" and that change in a "patient" is an illusion. Finally, we have become aware that our ideas of how one "gets better" are in need of serious revision. Certainly this is one of the themes that binds together the papers in this volume. And if this book has an underlying theme it is our undiscovered wholeness, our buried life. What Gestalt is about is how to peel away the layers of "stuff"—bodily tensions, tragedy and drama, soap opera, roles and games—that keep this essential self undiscovered.

II

The Gestalt Institute of San Francisco was formed in 1967 at the direction of Fritz Perls, who asked Dr. Bob Hall, his friend and protégé, to undertake its organization. An informal study group already existed, meeting at the home of Janie Rhyne, an artist living in the Haught-Asbury district. The intoxicating trip that was San Francisco in the flower-child period centered on the Haight and strongly affected the evolving Institute. "Do your own thing" was the ethos of the small group who met regularly in Janie's picturesquely crumbling mansion. Initially we conducted workshops open to all and held in her attic-studio or in Bob Hall's spacious home in Mill Valley. As the number of psychotherapy professionals attending the workshops increased, there was a demand for training. This was met by Bob Hall and Cyndy Sheldon's setting up an ongoing group at his home.

A freedom and exuberance characterized the Institute activities; the old rules were dead, only experience could create the new. The first business manager was a

San Francisco cab driver related to one group member. His managing was eccentric, and it ended when, after a personal dispute, he disappeared together with the entire Institute records. A subsequent manager was Jerry Rothstein, a graduate student in philosophy of considerable competence, who went on to become director of Fritz's Canadian Gestalt center at Lake Cowichan, British Columbia. The Institute, then and today, maintains a healthy skepticism toward authority and a lively taste for innovation and experimentation. Today for example, Institue affairs are managed by a three-person board, selected periodically by drawing names from a hat. The only test of fitness to survive being survival, the Institute continues to draw students and to have good attendance at its various functions.

In 1975 during a bantering meeting at which some members were telling of their personal and professional activities from Hawaii to West Germany, the editor thought: "Why not show others these fruits of the Gestalt tree? Here is the creativity that Fritz Perls talked about!" This is what is offered to you here: our own experieince, shared with mystics, clients, students, friends, family—the entire bright, exciting, tragic dualistic world. Our friend Ram Dass, for example, shared and shaped his karma with us, and now with you.

III

The art and science of the Gestalt approach has now been firmly established but not enshrined. In its eclectic acceptance of multiple paths to wholeness, it welcomes all who recognize the ultimate reality of experience. This would include such wide-ranging figures as Ram Dass, Oscar Ichazo, Werner Erhard, and Swami Muktananda, to list only a few names.

The practitioners of Gestalt have become influential agents of change in our society; our influence has moved far beyond office walls, beyond the parking-lot-encircled "couch canyons" of therapy, and into the ferment of the everyday world. At every level, this mode of dealing with reality is becoming useful. For myself, this comes as a great relief, since Gestalt formation is the way I have always thought. Now at last I don't have to feel a bit guilty about my lack of logical, sequential precision!

And now for one more introduction: We invite you to introduce yourself and become acquainted with us at the San Francisco Gestalt Institute, 1719 Union Street, San Francisco, California 94123.

JACK DOWNING

PART ONE

A Talk at the San Francisco Gestalt Institute

Ram Dass

I. AN ENCOUNTER WITH FRITZ PERLS

I want to tell you about my first encounter with Fritz Perls. I was invited by the Canadian Broadcasting Company to do a four- or six-hour television taping from which they were going to cut and get an hour or two of tape out of it. When I walked into the studio, there was a total Maharishi Mahesh scene set up for me—a platform with cushions and flowers and incense and stuff, which is somebody's trip but not mine. But it's somebody's trip, all right? So I just surrender, usually. (*Laughter.*)

I was just warming up, and I was starting to talk about, ah, *love*, as I recall. And the door opened, and in walked a gentleman with a beret, followed by his entourage. There was a bit of commotion, and I just went on talking. A bridge chair was brought up and placed right next to my seat, and this gentleman sat down. This was not what I expected, and I did not know who he was. So I figured maybe he was an elderly

This talk was edited by Dorothy Luttrell and Jack Downing.

man brought on to make the show more interesting. (*Laughter.*) I said, "Hello," and I just went on with my presentation. Then the first word I heard from this gentleman was "Bullshit!"

There's a certain way you deal with people in groups that are being obviously egocentric in the way they're carrying on, you know? You just look compassionate and you say, "Hello," and then you go on with your thing, you know? I did that and he said, "It's all crap!" Well, that was the second time. The television cameras are grinding away, I'm trying to go on, but it's not easy.

I began to suspect who he was, having heard about him, and I knew that he had an island in Canada. So I said, "Dr. Perls, how do you do. I'm Ram Dass," and shook his hand. I figured, at least we could introduce ourselves. Well, every sentence I tried to get out he attacked. Then it turned out that everybody in the audience was Fritz Perlsian. See? So pretty soon everybody was attacking. I mean, it was like throwing a Christian to the lions, right? It was an *incredible* scene.

This went on for maybe twenty or thirty minutes, as I recall, when I said, "My predicament is that I don't say what I'm trying to say well because it's new to me. I'm just learning it. It's a very delicate flower I want to share with you, but you won't give me the space to do it in, because you're so busy saying what you think the universe is, you won't let me share this thing." He said, "I know all about your goddamn flower."

So at that point there wasn't any possibility that I could go on. So I took up my *mala* [prayer beads] and I sat down and I closed my eyes and I started to do mantra. I just didn't say any more. The cameras were grinding, and hundreds of dollars were being used up. And I sat. And they all talked among themselves. And they were yelling at me, "You're afraid. You won't come out. You're afraid."

And I just did my *mala* and I kept saying to my guru, inside me, "I just don't know what the trip is, and whatever you're laying on me, fine, but I'm just gonna sit here." And after about ten more minutes of this, they discontinued the show. And we all got up and left. So that's my encounter with your professional father. And if you are much worse than Daddy, there's gonna be a lot of trips around the prayer beads. (*Laughter.*) I felt I owed that story to the memory of Fritz Perls.

I also heard a story about the last words Fritz Perls uttered before he died, which may or may not be true. I thought it was charming. I will tell you what I heard. He was in a hospital and he sat up in the hospital bed, although he had many tubes in him. The nurse came in and said, "Dr. Perls, you lie down this instant. You shouldn't be up like this." And he said, as I heard the story, "Nobody tells Fritz Perls what to do." And then he died. That's the story as I heard it. Is that correct?

MAN: Very close.

RAM DASS: Does anybody here know differently? That's pretty exquisite, you know. Of all the Tibetan stories I've heard of how great men have died, that's the farthest out I've heard in all my life.

MAN: He'd been rehearsing that line for years.

WOMAN: I wonder who the next person he tried it on was.

II. COLLECTING THE QUESTIONS

RAM DASS: Right. Right. Since we are a small group, we could start rapping now. I can give raps, I can talk indefinitely, by the way; but it would be nice to respond to whatever it is that's in *your* heads, particularly about why you would come to hear me. What are you doing here? What is it that I can do for you? I think this is the more important question for me because, as far as I'm concerned, everything I do is part of my teaching, my yoga, for myself. I'm only working for myself, to be quite honest. I'm not here as a social service.

QUESTION: What do you mean, work on yourself? What will we do for you?

QUESTION: I'd like to know what you could add to us as psychotherapists. That is, what elements would you add to psychotherapy?

RAM DASS: Okay, I'll get those. I can take in about ten questions, and then I can work.

QUESTION: I have a personal question. I'd like to have you say something about inner changes as you go along the spiritual path. I'll say something about myself. For about eight years I was into yoga and the whole meditation and growth trip. I took Arica, and since that training I've really been feeling very lost—without a guru or whatever. I just feel lost.

RAM DASS: Okay, I'd like to talk about the path and how to work on yourself.

QUESTION: I'll tailgate onto the last question because I also anticipated making big, enormous changes inside me. Now, I feel a sense of disconnection and loss. I've been listening to your tapes and getting very turned on, so my expectation is that I'm looking for a guru. And you're gonna be it. I had to get that out.

RAM DASS: I hear it, I hear it. . . . Yes?

QUESTION: I have a very close friend who is dying, and I'd like to talk about death.

RAM DASS: Okay. Any others?

QUESTION: As I was coming tonight, I was wondering *why* I was coming because, unless I have business here that pays me, I usually don't come to the city. I just decided that I had to come. I don't know why I'm here, though.

RAM DASS: Okay. Let me work with these, then. And that'll lead to some more. People have asked me before, "How do you feel about psychotherapy in view of the fact that you were a therapist? My answer sounds facetious but isn't really. My answer is: If Buddha was your therapist, you'd get enlightened, but if your therapist thinks she or he is a therapist, watch out!

Attachment and Perception

Now, as I understand our mutual predicament . . . no, since I don't know all of you in this room, let me just talk about *my* predicament. I have a theoretical understanding of the evolution of consciousness. And in my theoretical framework, I understand that there is a place in me that *knows*; that there is a place in me that is it *all*; that is *Buddha*; that is *enlightenment*; that is *full consciousness*. Intellectually, I also know that my behavior and my emotions and my self-consciousness and a lot of things about me are not consistent with how I would be were I always in that knowing place. In other words, I am *not* Buddha. Right? And the discrepancy that I notice between the two I attribute, again theoretically, to the veils that exist. These veils are called, from within the system that I work in, my attachments. Is that clear? Now, the predicament I have with attachments or desires or being attached to my desires is that, as any psychology student knows, motivation affects perception. And therefore my desires affect what I see. In a real sense I am only seeing my own projective systems, my own attachments in the world. The desires are the veils, and my attachments to my desires are also the veils. Any places I'm not attached, I wouldn't notice. For example, say you're driving across country and you're really hungry. You drive into a town and out the other end of the town. You could describe pretty well which restaurants, cafés, etc., were in the town; you'd have a hard time describing hardware stores.

I could sit in this group and I could give a lecture, and I could get out of it any number of things. I could have been here just for a hundred bucks. That would be my motivation, if that was what the trip was about. All right? I could be here for a seduction, in order to find out who I was going to bed with tonight. All right? And I've gone through all these, by the way. I'm just talking about my own history when I say these things. I could also be here out of a sense of obligation to the scientific community. Each of these has motivated me, and in each case that's all I got. A great, profound teaching could be available for me in this situation and still I couldn't get it, since my motivation and resulting perceptual set excludes this. As my teacher, not my guru, said, "When a pickpocket meets a saint, all he sees are his pockets." (*Laughter.*)

Let's take another example: When people are primarily sexually oriented, that is, when they're horny most of the time; they put people into the categories of who's makable, who's a competitor, and who's irrelevant. That's roughly the three categories. (*Laughter.*) Now a person like that would look at the world and see the whole world in sexual terms, and would teach that these are the relevant, important categories. Freud in some ways was a symbol of that; at least that is what Jung said about Freud. And Freud said something else about Jung. And everybody was talking about each other's projective systems. Right? Adler was doing the third chakra, Jung was doing the fourth chakra, Freud was doing the second chakra, and each was a master of his own chakra.

Can You Trust What I Say?

The thing is that it takes light, light, light to see clearly, without projection. I know my predicament, where I am in my own projective system; I still am a relatively unconscious being. I can teach intellectually how I know it would be were I something other than I am. But the problem with intellectual stuff is, it really doesn't do much good for people. I mean, it's just little stuff I collect up here in my head and put in other heads. Here in the West we can all get very good at that, very intellectually sophisticated about saying it well. Right? But what we transmit to each other is our *beings*. We don't transmit the intellectual concepts, which only are the vehicles for transmitting our beings. We really are sharing our own level of evolution as manifested in our chakras.

So I need to tell you a story. This story comes from Thurber's *The Thirteen Clocks*. It's sort of a caricature of a fairy tale. In this story, the prince has a desire: he wants to get the princess. She is being kept by a wicked duke. The wicked duke wants piles of jewels in order to let go of the princess. But the prince is broke, so he goes to this wise man and he says to him, "Ah, how am I going to get the bread to spring the princess?" Right? The wise man answers, "Well, I'll tell you. On yon mountain is an old hag. If you go up to the top of the mountain and come to this hag and tell her a very sad story, she will cry. The quality of her is that when she cries, she cries jewels. See? And you collect the jewels, take them back, and give them to the duke. He'll be happy and he'll give you the princess. See? The prince says, "Oh, wise man, how can I ever thank you? Thank you, thank you!"

He's about to leave and the wise man says, "By the way, excuse me one minute, but I must tell you one thing. There's a bit of a problem here. I am under a curse, and the curse works so that fifty percent of everything I say is wrong." (*Laughter.*) "And the additional part of the curse is I don't know which fifty percent it is. See? So I have given you the best wisdom I have to offer you, but I must warn you that it may be wrong."

Okay, well now that roughly is the predicament I am in. Like, the stuff that comes through me is sometimes coming from *this* level, and sometimes it's coming from *that* level, and sometimes it's coming from somewhere else, because I'm all different levels. Right now I'm all the different places I ever was and ever will be, and I'm just going in and out of these levels all the time. So I assume no responsibility for what I'm saying. (*Laughter.*) Right? I'm saying it because I'm saying it, no other reason. If you don't want to be here, don't be here. If you're here and I'm saying it and you listen, then that's your karmic predicament and you've got to trust your own heart. And if I'm saying bullshit, forget it! If it feels good, use it. And if you use it for a while and then you realize it's no good, throw it away. It's okay.

QUESTION: Do you sometimes have a hunch at a given moment? (*Laughter.*)

RAM DASS: Yeah, but see, that's the predicament I'm in. You don't know which level that is either. "It just keeps on going, mother lover." See? Okay.

Attachment to Acts

So that's why, in Patanjoli's Raja yoga, it says, "There is no giving and no receiving." Which is a far-out idea, because you think there should be giving and receiving. But it means "Don't get attached to being the giver—or the receiver!" There's merely the grain.

You need it, you eat it; I need it, I eat it. It's not my grain or your grain. It's God's grain. Or it's *the* grain. Or however you want to say it.

I want to tell you a samurai story. This samurai is a religious swordsman, and it is his duty, when his master is killed, to kill the killer of his master. That's part of the samurai code. And so, for two years, this guy looks for the killer of his master. And he finally finds him, and he unsheaths his sword and he goes to kill this man, as is his proper duty. And the man spits in his face. At which point the samurai sheaths his sword, turns, and walks away. And the man runs after him and says, "I was the killer of your master. Why didn't you kill me?" And the samurai says, "Because I got angry." Now what he's saying is, "Because I got attached to killing you." And the killing that comes out of attachment creates more suffering.

This is far out if you can start to work with the idea of attachment to acts, because in the Bhagavad Gita it says, "You do what you do but you are not attached to being the actor." The acts occur in the same way trees grow and water flows—that is, as the Tao, or harmonious part of the universe. So until you are at the stage where actions are simply and naturally occurring, as long as you're still busy thinking *you're doing it*, you are sending out a particular vibration. So if you're attached to your desires, to the notion that doing is where it's at, you're conveying your attachment to somebody else, right? You are attached to being the actor.

So now we're in that same predicament as before. For example, let's take me: If I'm not a realized being, should I be talking to you at all? See? If I'm not a realized being, should I ever give anybody food? If I'm not a realized being, should I live? Should I do anything, you know? And the situation is that I *am* in a body, I *am* an incarnation, and I can't *not do* it anyway. But whatever I'm doing, even if I'm sitting in a cave, I'm sending out a series of vibrations, and I-we are all interrelated with one another whether it's in time and space or not—we're just all interrelated.

Work on Yourself

So it turns out that the optimum strategy that you can use to fulfill the bodhisattva vow of relieving the suffering of all sentient beings is to work on yourself. See? There is reality. It turns out there's nothing else to do, right? The working on yourself may involve sitting with other people and talking. In other words, this is my yoga at the moment. Right? It isn't like I sit in my room in the morning and I do yoga so I can come out and do the day. The day *is* the yoga. This day's experience becomes the vehicle. In this sense, being here tonight *is* my exercise.

Many different people have come to me with questions and I would empty (which we'll talk about later), and I noticed that the same response kept coming out, no matter how varied the situations were. Somebody would say, "How do I deal with my employer?" and someone else would say, "How do I deal with my child?" and on and on, you know. And I thought, well, either I'm very naïve, because I'm just not noticing individual differences, or I am touching something that is behind all those things, right? Because I kept saying, "Work on yourself, work on yourself, work on yourself." Right? Like for example, "How do I deal with my child?" It seemed like what I was saying was, "If you will work on yourself, you will be as centered and quiet and present and open and compassionate and loving as you can capably be, which is the optimum environment for the child to grow itself. You will create a space in which the child can manifest."

For myself, right now I'm dealing with issues like power and fame and all of my desires that are elicited by the role I find myself playing now. Okay? And that's a very hot fire. It's a very hot yogic fire. Right? The interesting game is to work with that hot fire. Get as close to the fire as you can get, so you're just getting singed, you know, so you can smell the burning flesh. And stay right there. You can get very holy by going off to a cave. You can get amazingly holy. But it's what I call a cheap high. (*Laughter.*) It doesn't last very long. You come down again. All right?

Every Act Is a Teaching

So now we're beginning to deal with your personal questions. The confusion and the feeling of lostness is a part of the yogic path. You feel confused and lost just because you don't have a framework to see these feelings as process. Confusion and feeling lost are part of the process. You've identified "process" with formal methods and certain special experiential states, while actually the whole of life is "process." See?

Every act I live is seen as a teaching that's being given to me. My liver acts up every time I cat too much pizza or drink too much beer, right? and yogis don't do that, but I'm doing it. (*Laughter.*) Even as every pulse of my liver is saying: "Lousy yogi, lousy yogi." Right? (*Laughter.*) I'm just sitting with that, and I'm working with it. That's the stuff I've got to work with. And if it leads me into a depression, the depression is the stuff I've got to work with, right? But the question is, Which is the framework from which you work with it? See? And that brings us to the whole question of what is personality and what is psychotherapy about.

Am I dealing with the questions you're asking? (*Assent.*) Feel free to interrupt. (*He laughs.*) I forget

I'm talking to the Gestalt Institute. (*Laughter.*) But feel free not to interrupt. (*Laughter.*) You here?

MAN: Am *I* here? I feel here.

RAM DASS: Okay. (*Laughter.*) You had a look on your face and I thought you were maybe somewhere else. You were, huh? But I'm not wearing my glasses, so I can't even tell whether, you know, you're a man or a woman, except for the beard. (*Laughter.*)

The Therapist's Predicament

Okay. Now, you know, I'm getting into a Kahlil Gibran role now in society: "Oh, great wise being, you have been among us these many years," you know. "Tell us about trial bearing. Tell us about love." And it's very far out, you know, and you say, "Bluup." And they say, "Thank you." (*Laughter.*) You've got to keep a sense of humor about the whole predicament, because it would get absurd if you took it seriously. Usually, when people say to me, "You're my guru," I say to them, "Well, that's your problem." (*Laughter.*) I don't see it as my problem, because I'm not buying that person's head trip. The predicament about psychotherapy is roughly the same one as I have in that situation. Right?

Well, let me do the summary statement first. That is: The only, the *only*, conscious strategy that a therapist has available is *to work with himself* and to see the therapeutic interaction as an opportunity for himself to become more conscious. Because all you have to offer another being is your consciousness—that which is compassion and love. It's the same, if you will pardon the expression, the same gestalt. (*Laughter.*) And until you are that, until you are consciousness or are love, everything you're doing is slightly tainted anyway. Right?

So what we're doing is really just perpetuating or

sharing the illusion with one another, all the time. We have, in a sense, a leaderless situation, for the most part. In order to help ourselves out of this, all we can do is adopt a strategy of interacting through whatever vehicle, person, or situation happens to be out there. And the nature of the interaction will be I work on myself and you work on yourself. I am your karma and you are my karma. We are each other's environment, in order to work on ourselves.

The vehicle may be called "psychotherapy"; the vehicle may be the parent-child relation; the vehicle may be lectures. The vehicle may be anything. The vehicle may be selling gum in a pharmacy. It doesn't matter what the form of the human interaction is. That's what is far out to me: Buddha could be the local shoe repairman at this moment.

Are you all familiar with Florence Kluckholn's distinction between man *over* nature, man *in* nature, and man *under* nature in terms of a cultural breakdown? We clearly are the products of a man-*over*-nature, doing culture, where we use siddhi, the power of our mind, to control and master nature. Now we are into doing things to other people, for other people, and about other people. We're into rearing our children, changing people's behavior, doing this to that. As I started to change, I noticed that I felt less and less that I was involved in doing anything *to* anybody; I felt more and more that I was interacting with people, and things were *happening*. So I started to adopt a very different perceptual strategy.

I'm in the position where people come up to me and say, "Thank you for what you've done for me." But I didn't think I did anything. Okay? So I can say, "You're welcome." Or I could say, "I didn't do anything," which just makes them think I did it all the more but I'm humble. Right? There's no way to be straight. Nobody can hear the "I didn't do anything" response because in their projective systems I did something to them, or for them, or about them.

I started to notice in myself that as I did less and less, more and more was happening, to everybody. Because when I thought that I was doing something to somebody, my attitude was imposing a model on the other person of somebody who needed to have something done to them. That's what I mean by "If the therapist thinks he's a therapist, watch out." Because if the therapist thinks he is a therapist, by definition you must be the patient, since there're only two of you in the room, you know.

I have some heavy karma to work out from my old days as a therapist, because I really needed my patients to be sick. And then I needed them to feel they were getting better. And I needed them to need me, and I punished them when they got too healthy. You know? I watched that horror show for years. Now that I look back on what I did, I realize I helped to perpetuate the situation because I had such an ego investment in being a therapist. Right?

Karma and Therapy

The concept of karma has become a reality to me, not merely a theoretically interesting concept. And the way karma is a reality for me is that each individual is unfolding in an evolutionary sense and is working out, through his interactions with the environment, certain sets of predisposing factors. These are like the DNA code, except they're on a psychic plane rather than on a physical plane.

When I was a therapist, I was Freudian, psychoanalytically oriented; but I also knew I was selectively training my patients. I'd read the research that shows that Freudians end up with patients who are Freudianized, and Rogerians end up with people who are Rogerianized, and Adlerians end up with Adlerianized people, and so on. I knew damn well that if somebody came in and talked about, say, their economic problems and I was sitting there, you know, thinking about what I was gonna buy for dinner, and then they'd say, "Um, my mother had a lot of trouble with money, too." And I'd say, "Oh?" See how I was reinforcing the material that fit in with my Freudian theory that mother was what was wrong with them? Because as long as I was attached to my intellect being my tool for bringing about change in someone else, I had to have a computer program, a Freudian model to plug into my intellect-computer. I had to "know" what I was doing and how to do it and how it ought to come out.

But as I started to get into karma, I realized that I couldn't do much to anybody anyway. Because they were hung up where they were and, like the pickpocket, couldn't see anything else even if you could give them the ultimate wisdom. Let's assume you're given one question you can ask a fully enlightened being, my guru. So you say, "Maharaji, I'm only making thirty rupees a week. Would you call so and so, use your powers to get me thirty-two rupees?" Can you imagine that? It's like going to the king who has all the royal jewels and asking for a pass to the baseball game. (*Laughter.*) I mean, it's just absurd, you know? But you can see that people get caught in their own desire systems and that's all they see of what's available, right?

A fellow comes to see me and he's very severely arthritic. He's a young guy and he's all bent over. And it takes about three or four people to get him into the room and get him comfortable on cushions. And he's on a hundred aspirins a day. Right? He's really into it in a heavy way, right? Okay. I sit down and I look at him. Now we have a choice of what the name of the game is going to be at that point. In his situation, everybody's involved with his predicament. You almost can't help but get involved with his predicament, see? But I'm sitting, emptying and emptying and emptying. And what I see is another being just like me who is in a heavy karmic runoff. Right? It's just like you're driving a new Lincoln Continental and you pass an old Volkswagen that's going on two cylinders, just clunking along. And you look over and you know there's just the difference—not better or worse, just different.

In India I watched and heard Maharaji. The higher I got, the more I got the teachings. The more I emptied my models of who he was and how he was working, the more profound the teachings were as they poured through me. I saw the individual differences in what everybody was getting from him. And I thought, "Well, he's not getting bugged by it. He's just being. He's just being a statement of himself. And everybody's getting what they can from him." And that started to get me on to this other model, right? And this model says, "Leave people alone. Start to honor karma the way it is." Karma comes out of a religious, spiritual connectedness for me now. It's really the concept of "not my will, but Thy will, O Lord."

As I look around now, I see divine plan. I see the plan of the universe. It's not law in the rational, linear, analytic sense. It's more like the Tao, or the natural law of the universe. I can see that it's all lawfully related. You can follow it through in physics or biogenetics or chemistry and you will get back to incredibly, exquisitely simplistic kinds of structures in the universe. And I began to see that all of it was lawfully unfolding. All of it is just lawfully unfolding. And getting back to the Kluckholn man-*in*-nature idea, I was becoming part of that lawful unfolding. All right? And all I had to do was become part of it, to play my part and let each person do what they do. My merely being around, being an environment in which they do it, and the way I function in the environment is a statement of my unique karmic predicament. It happens that I'm a teacher, whether I like it or not. I can stop teaching as often as I want; I keep ending up as a teacher. I gave up teaching at Harvard; I gave up teaching after psychedelics; I keep giving it up and it keeps coming back. But each time, it's with less attachment.

In therapy I began to entertain the possibility of not having a model of who my client ought to be other than who they are at the moment, or a model of how this interaction ought to come out. See? Take the therapist's model of "craziness." In the old psychedelic days, the first thing that was laid upon us was "What are you doing with these drugs? Don't you see some people go into mental hospitals?" The problem was I would see a kid after he'd been six months in a mental hospital and he would be more together afterwards than I ever would have predicted he would have gotten in the next forty years, in therapy or just bungling along on four out of eight cylinders, you know? And in a way, that kind of total drug flip-out was one of the great liberating forces in his life. So I started to think, maybe everybody should go "crazy." Now I don't know.

Imposing Models

I started to stop having such strong models about how it all *ought* to be for the changes to occur, because I realized I didn't know so damn much. I stopped trying to play God and began to let go of my desire of how I thought you should be. And I started letting you be how you are and merely being with you as consciously as I could be. And more and more I let the interaction be "we meet, and . . . ?" This is all very harmonious with the Gestalt philosophy, I would imagine.

Now, when I sit with an individual who comes to see me, here's what happens. I just sit there, centering. I just am quiet, just quiet. And then they do this thing. They go "bluub." Right? They lay out their predicament. They tell me their story line. They tell me their melodrama. They tell me who they think they are and how they think it is. All right?

Now, my attachment to thought is very minimal at this point. Because I think thoughts are just thoughts, and that the structure of the ego—I may be using a sacred term here; if I am, I apologize (*laughter*)—the structure of the ego is a structure of conceptualization, really, which includes feelings and so on. It's really a cognitive map, if you will, of who I am and who you are and how it all works. And each person is laying their map out, which includes who I am. All right?

If you look out at another person when you're horny, as I said, you see who's makable or irrelevant. Let's say you're a scientist looking at bodies. You might do a Sheldon somata typing of another person. And you'd see an ectomorph, a mesomorph, or an endomorph. Okay. You flip the switch once, and now the world has become all personality, because that's who you think you are. And somebody says, "Who are you?" And you say, "Well, I'm a reasonably happy person," or "I'm achieving a lot," or "I'm creative," or "I'm depressed," or "I'm realized." These are all personality terms, for the most part.

If you flip one more little flip on the game board, then the world is made up of twelve permutations and subtleties thereof, and you can do the astrological trip and then you see a Libra or an Aries. And for somebody who is in that domain, that's the world. That's it.

That's the reality of it. And everything is explicable within that system.

I'm not putting down systems. You can use one system to get rid of another system. Then all you've got to do is get rid of the system you used to get rid of the first system. Okay? And that's true of all methods, so it's nothing sacred. If you do one more flip, then when you look in the eyes of another person you're looking through the veil of body, sex, and differences in culture. You're looking through the veil of personality, which has been very sacred to many of us. You're looking through the veil of astral identity or what would be called archetypal identities or subtle body identities.

Brotherhood Is a Reality

And what you see when you look in the eyes of another person is another person looking back at you. And it's like, "Are you in there?" (*Laughter.*) And it's two identical beings inside two different packages meeting. The individual differences are in the packaging, not in the entities themselves. And you're looking at another entity. Right? And you'll recognize each other, and your reality space becomes entities, not individual differences among entities. And at that point the whole business of "we" and "them" falls away. And that's where brotherhood becomes a perceptual reality, not an intellectual overlay. You hear what I'm saying? So that, at that point you're talking to another being just like yourself and it becomes a world of *us*, even if the other person looking out is seeing you and themselves in personality. Okay. You hear what I'm trying to say?

It's not that Buddha is going to come with the begging bowl and orange robes and say, "I'm Buddha, may I come in and enlighten you?" You know? It could be that you go around the world and you join this and do that, and it turns out all the time it was your Aunt Tillie cooking chicken soup, waiting for you to get back. And when you do get back and have cleared your vision so that you're not caught up in the symbols of holiness or symbols of consciousness, you look and there's this being of light and love and compassion, and she says, "I've been waiting for you. Have some chicken soup." The situation is, most of us wouldn't see Buddha if we walked over him. Because we're too busy looking for Buddha, you know? And that's our predicament.

So when I sit down in a therapy situation with another person, who I'm sitting down with is another being just like me who has their karmic trip just like I have my karmic trip. Where is the criterion about which trip is better than any other trip? See? That's the predicament. It's a very subtle issue.

The Sea of Ignorance

I know that my perception is limited. I'm faced with the predicament that I don't know why it all is the way it is or how it's supposed to come out. So in the sea of ignorance that I'm sitting in, what do I do? See? Do I impose a model, the best model of how I think it ought to come out? Or do I listen? Instead of taking the stance that I know, I take the stance that I don't know —and that I'm listening to hear what part I'm supposed to play with another person. See?

In 1954 at Stanford, when I was a graduate student, I had my first therapy patient. Vic Lovell, whom some of you know, was my first therapy patient. After I had "therapized" him for a few years, he took pity on me and turned me on to pot. And that started a lot for me. So who would have predicted that? Who would have predicted, when I was a professor at Harvard, that seven years later I would be sitting on a mountaintop in a dress, fasting and following my breath? (*Laughter.*) I couldn't have predicted it in 1961. Then the word "yoga" was a joke to me.

So I don't know the game. All right? I don't understand what I'm doing or who I am or where it's supposed to go. And what has happened is that I don't care, see? That's the blasphemy in the Western model. I don't care, because I don't think I have to know who the hell I am—or what I'm doing. And when I meet another person, I don't have to know what our interaction is supposed to result in. That's none of my business. (*Laughter.*) I just have to quiet down enough to be whatever I am in the situation and whatever will happen will happen. Right?

This is related to power and whether or not I need the personal power of thinking that I know what's going to happen and that I'm doing something to somebody. I take a much more passive stance, where I am, in effect, merely a part of a process and am just interacting. Sometimes they say, "I think you're full of bullshit!" and get up and walk out. Well, that's interesting. And that's as interesting as when they say, "Thank you. You've changed my whole life," and go out smiling. See? Because we all know how to give a cheap high as well as anybody else does. And I can get everybody off, so that at the end of an evening they all come up and say, "Ohhh! Thank you, it was wonderful!" And tomorrow it's just as shitty as it was yesterday. See? Getting high together isn't what the game is all about. It's more interesting than that.

Attachment to Your Own Story Line

I had to digress to these flips of the thing to show you that when I'm looking at another person what I'm seeing is another person looking back at me. But what they're seeing is their stuff. And their stuff is coloring the picture. Returning to my story about the arthritic man, the question is: Am I going to be caught in his picture of himself as an arthritic and merely be somebody who's pitying his predicament? In which case we would both get lost in the stuff. Or am I going to say, "Well, hello in there. It must be a heavy trip. Are you working with it? How is it? Is it interesting being arthritic?" You know?

A woman comes to me and she says, "My daughter's run away and she took drugs and she's gone." She says, "I've been a bookkeeper, and my husband left me when the baby was six months old and I've spent my whole life working to support this child and her sister and now she went off to the South and she's forged a check of her sister's and . . . " The whole thing is maudlin, grotesque, sad. You can see the woman working as a bookkeeper for twenty years and the whole thing, you know? And she gets all done, and I've heard every single word she said, and I say, "Right." See? Like, you've told me the whole story line, now what? And then there is silence. She says, "Well, you don't understand." She felt she hadn't gotten the proper response out of me, so she went through the whole story again. See? And I said, "Right, I hear you. And here we are. Now what? What does your program say happens next? If you'll tell me the script, I'll play. But otherwise, here we are; we're two beings, and you've got your trip. Do you want to hear my trip? My trip's as poignant as your trip." (*Laughter.*)

A famous black musician and I were stoned on something or other and we were driving into New York City. He was coming on ferociously about white bastards and the whites and all of this persecution paranoia. And I said, "Man, you bleed a lot." And he says, "Hey, don't come on to me man, I'll beat the shit outtaya, you white mother-fucking son of a bitch." And I said, "Do you realize that I could have something that could be as much of a drag as you have?" He says, "What could you have? What are you, a Jew? So—big deal. You don't have it bad like the blacks have." I said, "Listen, for years I've been hung up on being homosexual. That was my big problem for fifteen to twenty years." He said, "You got a *problem*!" (*Laughter.*) See, it was like I'd outdone him at the game of things to be pitied for, you know? And from then on, we had a straight relationship. (*Laughter.*) As straight as we could get, I mean. (*Laughter.*)

And that gets us back to the question of whether you think you're a therapist and whether the patient has to think they're a patient or not, right? What I'm seeing is another person who has their story line, of which I'm a part. And I have a story line, of which they're a part. But I'm *not* attached to my story line and they *are* attached to their story line. And the question is how long that attachment will last; because the minute you're not attached to your story line, then you're free to change it or then it is free to change.

Free Will and Determinism

And that brings me to one more little digression (*he laughs; a few others chuckle*), and that's the issue of free will and determinism. (*Laughter.*) Which we could handle very simply by saying, "Is there free will or is there determinism?" In the old days, when I was a social scientist, I said very wisely to my classes and they wrote it down, "Well, it's all determined." (*Laughter.*) And before that, when I was a romantic, I said, "It's all free will." And I said that with the same amount of conviction with which I had said the other thing. And now my answer is "There is free will and it is all determined," and I say that with the same amount of conviction.

As far as I can see, at this moment the answer is both. Every day you get up and you decide whether to wear the green sweater or the brown sweater, and you think you'll go to the toilet now or go after you drink your orange juice. And you think you're making decisions. And you make them, and that's free will. On that plane free will exists, obviously, because you're doing it, every day.

As you quiet down and go inside and inside, you come to a place where you see the exquisite design of the game. And you begin to see that though your thoughts appear to be from within and involve free choice, from another place they are obviously part of the law and are determined. There isn't anything outside of the law, including gurus and gurus' grace. Now, as you become more conscious, the game is not to advance from one plane to the next plane, rejecting the first plane. The game is ultimately to live on all planes simultaneously, so that you are practicing free will knowing that there is no free will.

One Consciousness in All Things

And you live with paradoxes. And living with many paradoxes simultaneously is part of becoming conscious. And one of the additional paradoxes is that if you flip the thing once more, you look at another person's eyes and what you see is a mirror and you're looking back at yourself. And you realize there is only one of it.

Separation is a veil. Looking at another is consciousness looking at itself. And it is *just* consciousness. The whole thing is consciousness embedded in all these things. So each of us is just a set of eyes looking out from this one thing—consciousness.

If you go one step further you begin to have a unitive experience—an awareness of the oneness of the universe or the fact that it's all one consciousness. The entire universe can be conceived of as energy, and a synonym for "energy" is "consciousness" at that point. It is not self-consciousness, but it *is* consciousness. And that domain where you merge, you become one, is where all the miracles come from. And that's where your identity is located, not in separateness or individual differences but in the awareness of one consciousness in all things.

Self: A Set of Processes

Western science is coming very close to what Buddha saw. Buddha said that ultimately there aren't any "things" in the universe, there's merely process. There is no self, there's merely a set of processes that appear to be a self. There's nobody there. You are now a different being than you were a second ago. Because of the way you're looking, self looks constant. But in fact, self is a changing thing.

Buddha said, "When you go back, inside yourself, behind, behind, behind, behind, behind, behind, behind, behind . . . you get to the point where you go behind your own thought. You see thoughts coming, existing, and dying." And this is far out, because at that point, when you're in that plane of reality, you are no longer in time; that is, you're in a plane which is behind time. Since everything in the universe is lawfully related, that which is about to happen is the same as that which has happened. It all lawfully exists already, were you able to stand back and see it. Okay?

How Do We Learn?

QUESTION: From what point of view are you describing this—from the point of view of a person who has felt it or as a person who has been told about it and read about it?

RAM DASS: I hear the question. (*Very long pause.*) There are three ways in which you begin to function as if something is valid. The first is you've had a direct experience of it. The second is that somebody you know and trust has had a direct experience of it and they tell you it's so. And you trust what they say because you know that they're straight because you know them to be. And the third is that you've read it and it fits in with your rational system. This is a weaker way, but it's still one we use a lot. Almost everything I know now is some interaction of these three. Right? I couldn't clearly say it's one or the other. I'm not copping out; I'm going to deal with your question, but I'm trying to tell you the shades of it. I've stopped trying to figure out where each thing comes from.

For example, I had hundreds of acid trips in which I experienced certain things. But because I had no conceptual model for understanding them, these experiences just went inside me and sat there. Now, I will be studying some old tome, a Hindu scripture or some Buddhist scripture, and suddenly I'll come across something that clarifies that experience: "Oh, that's what that was. Oh, far out." See?

So what's happening is that I'm sitting with a whole set of undigested experiences that as yet have no conceptual framework for digesting them. But often what comes in from reading, or from my guru, or from other beings, resonates with some of this stuff, whether I intellectually grab hold of it or not, and it gives me a feeling of the validity of it. All right? So in some way I'm trying to share with you the levels at which I know certain things.

Spiritual Powers

QUESTION: Would you say something about spiritual powers, like clairvoyance? Have you had any such experiences?

RAM DASS: Now, I have been what seems to me thus far to be blessed by having no spiritual powers. Right? Because to get to use spiritual powers along the way is very seductive. I have, however, had the experience of going into the plane where I have seen future events, but I have no control over it. I have then come back from that plane and, in fact, those events I saw have come to pass. But what has happened is that I interpret it on this plane as an interesting hallucination or an interesting theoretical possibility because, when I come back from that plane, I'm not the same person. In other words, I don't act on the basis of it. And when the event happens, I say, "Isn't that fascinating?" But since I have no control over it, it hasn't been very relevant in my universe.

I have had certain direct experiences with spiritual powers, but just little ones—just little baby ones. For example, I know something's going to happen, or I know a certain person's going to call me, or something like that. But I've never studied it, nor have I ever attempted to deal with it in a systematic way.

It's a place in me that subtly happens, so that when my guru told me something that was going to happen, it happened. It was like show biz. I mean, my guru was just so in control of the scene. Of the future. Do you hear what I'm saying? I'm trying to deal with the way the thing becomes valid for me, all right? And even though I may not have that power, I'm living with a guy who does. Right? And I'm seeing a universe that puts me into that reality.

Emptying

QUESTION: What do you do when you do that, when you do that motion [running *mala,* prayer beads, through your fingers]? Many times, after you finish saying something, you hold your head as though you were reading notes there.

RAM DASS: Well, in this particular case, what I'm doing is tuning to my mantra. I'm just going empty. I'm emptying and then—phoomp—and then I start. The *mala* comes back in again because all the stuff that's been programmed by your questions is still unresolved. It's still sitting, needing resolution. But at that moment I was just emptying, and it's just a peculiar bodily pattern of mine that I do it that way. Right?

MAN: It looked like you were reading notes.

RAM DASS: Yeah. Well. (*Laughs.*) They're very subtle notes. (*Everybody laughs.*)

So if people come and treat me as Kahlil Gibran and ask me what I do, the answer is: "If you'd like the secret of my game, I empty." I don't try to think of the answer anymore. I used to try to think of the answer because I was using my intellect as my only vehicle. Now I talk words, but I talk words like a guitarist plays music. It's just "bluuuhhh," like you're hearing now. I'm just sitting inside going "rama, raaaama, raaaaaamaa," and this is happening. No doing, no thinking, and this is happening—including a "bluuuhhh." This is happening.

To give you a little tighter explanation, if you think that one might be difficult: Most of you are all familiar with driving cars, I'm sure, and the knowledge that you drive a car on base brain. Most of the time, when you're driving a car, you may be playing the radio, smoking a joint, looking through the window to see if the cops are following you, and watching your speedometer while talking to somebody. I mean, there are a number of things going on at the same time you're making these incredibly complex distinctions about centrifugal and centripetal force and rate and stuff. If you tried to use your intellect to drive the car while all this was going on, it would blow you apart. But it's all working perfectly. And it's all base-brain stuff. It's just happening.

Well, it gets so that your thinking processes are going on, even your creative thought processes, at that same level. And you sit in the space behind those thought processes and you watch thought happen. So that when a person asks me a question, I just go back into the mantra and empty. And out of this place comes whatever comes. And I have less attachment to my words than I used to. Right? Now . . .

QUESTION: Could you explain "empty?"

RAM DASS: Empty?

MAN: Yeah. Just how you "empty."

RAM DASS: There's another way of talking about the emptying process, the going back inside, that is very productive. You may have seen a book called *Cutting Through Spiritual Materialism*, by Chögyam Trungpa. If you haven't, it's a very, very useful book. He's a profound being. And he talks about the spaciousness of situations. He uses the word "spaciousness." And that's roughly the same thing as the emptying process. In the Aparmetrasutra it says, "form is emptiness," and then it says, "emptiness is form." Now, what we've been talking about is the seeing of forms in the universe and then extricating yourself from the attachment to having to see those as forms, until you realize that all the forms are coming out of emptiness. Right? The forms are really empty.

Like, each person's story line is just that person's story line. And it's just a story line; it's like a cloud going by; it's just stuff. It's just empty stuff. You begin to see the stuff of the universe as also empty. You look at your own body, and if you do certain meditations, your whole body turns into just electrical energy and you can feel it going through changes all the time and you realize it's a constant changing.

So, as you're looking at the universe, you begin to see it all as falling into nothing, as it were, a going into emptiness. And you begin to see that form is empty. See? The predicament is that when you get to that place which is called *shunyata*, or the emptiness of it all, you're still only part-way home. If you're attached to emptiness, that's just another form you got stuck in, that's still an attachment. So you can't sit there either. See? So the next step of the game is where they say nirvana and samsara become one. That is, you come back into the form, but you are simultaneously in the emptiness. See?

And that's what I'm telling you about living with paradox—living with the paradox of free will and determinism, living with the paradox of emptiness and form. So that you're living your life in a world made up of forms in which you're playing your part as a form. Your personality is here and your body is here, and you do all these things with bodies and with personalities and all this stuff, while, at the same moment, nothing is happening because it's all empty. See?

With that recognition there comes a space such that when an act occurs, it's as if the act is coming out of the void and going back into the void. That is, there's a certain spacious, timeless quality, like you're sitting in a place that is behind time.

And you're not watching in a "dissociation in the service of defense" kind of way; it's not a dissociative process. It's *simultaneous,* because you're also in it. You're not not-in-it in order to be out of it. You're not out of it because of anxiety. You are simultaneously in it and out of it. That's what I have to convey to you: that you're totally with your feelings and you're in your life and you're in your body and you're doing a thing, but, at the same moment, there's all this space around it.

Paradox and Dualism

QUESTION: Evidently these last few remarks of yours are an explication of the phrase "living with paradox." You seem to mean the moment-to-moment recognition of, and awareness of, the facts of paradox. Is that what you mean by living with paradox?

RAM DASS: Um . . . there are stages. And one of the stages is where you try to make sense out of everything. So you try to deny the paradox. Then comes the recognition that there *is* paradox; and then you are sequentially living in one or the other side of it. You keep flipping back and forth and noticing the paradox. Then there is another stage, where you-they come together, so that you're not consciously thinking "paradox" anymore, but your life is living with both sides of the paradox simultaneously, each of them as intimately related to you as the other. You're not in one or the other, because it would be in one that the other would seem paradoxical. Do you understand what I'm saying?

MAN: Isn't that another form? I won't pretend that I do understand, but you're on tape and to save time we'll just have to go over it later.

RAM DASS: Well, no, I wouldn't like you to do that,

because you've been with it thus far and I wouldn't like you to lose it now over that question.

MAN: Well, I think, for me, the point is fine enough that I'd be happy to hear you say it again.

RAM DASS: Well, okay. When you say "living with something," that's almost a sloppy term, because "living with" implies a dualistic relationship to something. A split. No gestalt. That means, *I'm* "living with" *that*. Meaning the paradox is *over there* and I'm *over here*. That's a stage, a point on the continuum of development.

There is a later stage, where you *are* the paradox, where the paradox is manifested *through* you. So that every act as a being becomes more conscious. Every act, across the whole spectrum, every act is harmonious with every plane of reality. There is no act which makes sense here but also does not make sense there. There is no paradox. It makes sense here and makes sense there because you are both here and there at the same moment. And you are also, if you'll remember the emptiness-form paradox, neither here nor there. That's the additional paradoxical element that we can notice as we come down to talk about it.

In terms of action, the conscious being is a mass of paradox in behavior. As the observer, you would notice the paradox looking from outside in, but from inside, as the experiencer, you are . . . like, well, people say to me, "You are very loving"—but I'm not experiencing being loving. I did for a long time, but now, in fact, I'm *becoming* whatever that "being loving" is. There's no longer an *experiencer* of love. The subject and object come together—there's that thing (*clapping sound*) that happens. That's why the Zen monk goes around *just* washing the dishes. There's nobody saying, "I'll wash the dishes." There's *just* washing dishes. There's *just* walking. There's *just* chopping wood.

There's *just* living life, if you will, without that separate self-consciousness. And that awareness of the paradox is still within the dualistic framework. It's still *somebody* noticing *something*. So it is a stage. And you are right that it happens. But that isn't the ultimate place. All right?

III. LOVE

MAN: Ram Dass, is personal relationship important to you now? By personal relationships, I mean intimate, erotic, romantic relationships, in the sense of one person being special.

RAM DASS: No. (*Very long pause.*) I can't tell when I say "no" what stage I'm saying "no," or who's saying "no." All right? As recently as last summer I had anticipated that I was going to be married. Right? And the woman I was going to be married to was somebody my guru was calling Mrs. Ram Dass. Right? That's how much it looked like it was an inevitability. And then, at a certain point in the dance, it just became further apparent that that wasn't our work at the moment. I can only describe what I'm experiencing without going into a psychological description of where that might be coming from, but that was the feeling.

There was a stage where I was experiencing unbearable love for every human being I looked at. I mean the kind of love that made me want to have each person as my lover. See, I went through going from a homosexual to a bisexual dance, where, since people were turning on to me and opening, I suddenly saw all these lovers. And I was—I never had enough, so I was collecting, you know? And everybody was a potential because I wasn't living in the world where only half of the population was possible. From my own sexual what-do-you-call-it, pathology or karma or whatever you want to call it, everybody was a possible lover, you know. So that I was like . . . um . . . I was like (*he chuckles*) a drunk in a liquor factory. I couldn't decide —a little of this, a little of that, you know. And I was collecting and collecting.

So what happened was that I started to get very confused, because in our culture we have certain expectations of what you do with somebody you love that intensely. I'd get on a bus and I'd walk down the aisle of the bus and I'd look at somebody and I'd be drunkenly in love with them and I'd want to throw myself in their arms or say "hello," and they knew it too, you know. What're we gonna do about it? If it happens to be an old woman with a shopping bag who's going home from work, and she's got her family, what're we gonna do, start a whole thing, you know? (*Laughter.*) And there's nothing to do. So you just look and say, "Hello, hi ya," and that's it.

I had gone through this interesting scene with Tim Leary some years back. I was guiding LSD trips, and those of you that have worked with LSD know that when a person opens and they've never opened before, they look at you with a kind of love they've never experienced before. And at the end of the trip, you are like a lover to them. All right? People at the end of the trip would say, "I love you. I've never loved anybody like that." And my needful self would be terribly pleased by that. They would say, "Can I be with you next week?" and I'd say, "Well, Tuesday let's be together." And the next week, I'd run another session and the same thing would happen with somebody else, and then that would be Wednesday night. So I got up to about six sessions and I went to Tim and I said, "Well, I guess you can't run any more than seven sessions in your life. I haven't room for more lovers, really. I've got every night booked."

Tim was the one who helped me by giving me the Taoist way of perceiving it, saying, "There's another level from which to do it." He showed me the reading from the *Book of Tao* which says, "The leader who leads the worst, people pay. The next better leader, they fear. The next better leader, they love. And with the best leader, they think they did it all themselves." See? And that desire to be loved was creating in them that "I love you" space. All I had to do was give up that desire and then the thing would fall away.

And the minute that I did that, it did. Right? The minute I let go of the needful quality in me, there was a different kind of love. The difference between my desire for interpersonal, romantic love, which has the love-hate polarity in it, and what would be called conscious love or Christ-love is that the latter is not a possessive love or a needful love.

In Love

If I may be allowed one more Kahlil Gibranism, it appears that when people are "in love" with one another, what in effect is happening is that the person that they are "in love" with is, from an instinct-theory point of view, the key stimulus that allows the release of the connection between themselves and the place *within them* where they are love. That is, you are my connection to the place in me where I am love. And then I am *in* love. Which means I am in the space, I am in the plane of reality, that is love. And you're my connection to tune to that place where I am love.

Being *in* the love reality changes my whole perception of everybody, and I start to see everything as beautiful when I'm turned on. And I get hooked on my love connection in the same way a junkie gets hooked on his or her connection. And the idea that my connection may have other clients, if they're a guru or therapist or whatever, or might turn away gets very frightening because I'm so needful of that connection. But what I'm connecting to is a place in myself. Right?

If, on the other hand, I have been able to use other techniques, which I can also get hooked on, as my connection to go into this love space, the game is ultimately that I *become* the love space. I merge into that space. And I become, in effect, love. I am love itself.

That's the game—that's the difference. I'm no longer "loving" as a verb—I am the state itself. At that point, every one of my perceptions is that of a lover, even though it is not connected to an external input (another person) that elicits it. All right? I'm just in the love place. And then I'm in love with everybody I meet. Whether they are in love with me or not, I am in love with them. See? I'm in the place of love and they're welcome to come if they can come. That's up to them. Into love, right? (*Laughter.*)

Now I'm beginning to experience that space most of the time because I'm a symbolic statement of a vibrational place in a person which allows them to touch that love place they often can't touch by themselves. You hear what I'm talking about? From in inner experiential point of view, I'm not clinging to "being loving" anymore; whether you'd say I'm fulfilled and don't need it or I'm too neurotic for close relationships, I can't tell you. I can't tell you where it's coming from. All I can say at this moment is that I just move from space to space to space, and every human being is like every other human being.

Erotic Love

You ask about erotic love. When I'm making love to somebody, it's hard to describe. (*Very long pause.*)

It is incredibly rich, in the sense that it's all the little levels; it's obviously the kinesthetics, it's obviously the fantasies, it's obviously the psychological sensuality, it's obviously the interpersonal thing, and it's obviously the yin-yang, and it's obviously and obviously and obviously and it's totally empty. Right? It's all of those at once. Right? And you can't push any one away or try to grab of the ignorance where it's only one thing and not another. Nor can you make it empty, because it's all the other stuff too, right? And that's more and more of every act for me now.

What you begin to realize is that it gets to the point where you're starting to enter into a state that is almost like being in the orgasmic moment at all moments. See? But its not *not-experiencing*—it's the merging. It's the place where you go *beyond* experience. (*Pause.*) All right, I'm trusting it for me; I'm just telling you about the little places in answer to your question. All right?

There are some people who are so remotely connected —they are so much cut off from the inner place in them where they are this higher consciousness—that the only route that's available to them is through an outside form. And for those people, sometimes it works that an external being can awaken in them that kind of love. It's divine love which starts out as interpersonal love— an interpersonal devotion and respect for somebody who's wiser and very loving and very present. And they open to that person in a way they couldn't open to themselves because of the model they have of who they think they are, right?

And the quality of one of these beings is that because they have no attachments, in a sense they are like mirrors. They're just very clear. And so you don't get a negative reply—you send your paranoid projection in and it vanishes because there's nothing that feeds it coming from the other person. All that comes back is love and presence and so on. So you can cut through a lot of your own stuff through being around one of these very clear other beings.

Attachment to Your Guru

Now, what happened to me was how I felt when my guru came along and blew my mind. He told me things he had no way of knowing, so he intellectually blew my mind. Then I experienced this tremendous wrenching and opening of the heart and this love, and so I was drunkenly in love with, and intellectually blown out by and relating to—at this new, deeper level—this old man in India. Right? And I hung around him, and in the whole time I was in India the first trip I saw him maybe an hour and a half in all. That's as much as I got from him. Little moments of ten minutes each and maybe one of an hour when we drove up to the mountains. Out of all that interaction came *Be Here Now* and all the stuff that I did after that for years. Right? That's how little it was involved with the actual time-space thing.

When I came back in 1970, we were all changed. A new production—The Arrival of the Westerners—had been staged, and suddenly there were a lot of Westerners there. Before, I was alone, and suddenly, all these people were crowding in and taking over his consciousness, so I didn't get as much as I was used to getting. I went through the jealousy and all of the stuff that the little trailers around a guru go through—anger and competitiveness and Who's gonna get the apple? and stuff like that. And I went on changing, and then I got to the point where I realized that it wasn't the body and the apples and all that; that wasn't what it was any longer.

And I was going to meet him on an astral plane because he kept saying, "Meditate on me and do a guru mantra right here." He meant for me to do this whenever I wanted to be connected with him. So I figure, when I'm right in front of him, instead of getting hooked into all this crap of taking apples and cinnamon, I'll meditate on my *ajun*. I'll just ignore him physically, and I'll connect with him on another plane and use the energy of this situation.

Nonattachment to Your Guru

And then, after a while, I saw that connection was another shuck, okay? That it was like the Chinese boxes, each inside the other, like infinite doorways, and I just kept going through and through and through. I gave up one attachment and I picked up another. And one day, I'm sitting across the courtyard from him and everybody's rushing around him. I'm not even over there with the crowd anymore, you know? And I'm thinking, "This is nothing. What is this thing? It's not that guy in the blanket, and it's not his astral being. There's nothing to go to get it. It's not anybody out there. I don't need to ever see him again. I don't care if I never see him again." Right?

And just as I'm thinking this thought, an old man rushes over from the other side of the courtyard and he touches my feet. And I said—I honor him—and I said, "Ah, Babaji, why did you just touch my feet?" And he said, "Maharaji said, 'You go over and touch Ram Dass's feet because he and I understand each other perfectly.' " And what he was doing at that moment was giving me license to realize that he wasn't it. Right? And right after that I left and I never saw him again, because he left his body before I came back to India.

I never missed him after he went. Here's my connection to whatever game it is that I seem to be involved in and he dies (*snaps his fingers*). And at first there was no reaction. I thought, "Uh-oh, no guilt reaction, no grief reaction, must be repression, watch it," you know. I went to India immediately, and I was crying for two weeks. And everybody said, "Oh, look at him, he's feeling so bad." I was blissing out, *that's* what was happening. Because it's like the Bible says, "Where two are gathered in my name, there I am." These people were all there with this intense love for this being. And I was just blissing out; I was just sobbing with bliss. There was not a moment of loss or sadness or anything, because he had weaned me from attachment to the form, right?

But for my purposes, it was useful to go through a being, a guru, to his physical presence, to get back to myself. Now if that being isn't pure, you might get caught in loving his person rather than realizing *you're* it, also. So it comes back on you. See, the beauty of my guru was that he didn't encourage my dependency on loving him—that's why he kept sending me away all the time. He didn't suck me into that dependency thing, right?

The Inner Teacher

Already many people in America have had a series of experiences that have opened them to possibilities, so they don't need the initial thing that a guru often does for people. That's already happened through acid or through the culture at this point. And they're ready —their faith is strong enough for them to connect inside to that inner teacher. The guru, God, and self turn out to be the same thing.

So there is, in you, the guru. And when you know how to do it, you listen. You listen to hear and then the thing comes from a deeper place in you. And then it's as if the inner guru was using you to do the thing. And more and more you feel like "not my will but Thy will be done"; you become an instrument of this deeper thing, which is not only "Thy," it's "I" also. But since it's not the one you often identify with your "self," it feels like "Thy" until those two come together. All right? So, for many Westerners, they are working with the inner guru rather than the external guru. Okay?

Spiritual Practices

QUESTION: Would you say something about practices—the yogi practice, method, and all of that?

RAM DASS: Each person has their own unique karmic predicament. Therefore, each person is going to have to find his own way. There are traditional methods, and you can go and explore them, and some of them may feel right to you and some of them may not. Only you can figure out whether or not it's working for you. If you have a guru, the guru can tell you, or you get to the point where you learn to listen to your intuitive sense of the rightness of the next thing you're doing for your journey.

At first, you're just beginning to have a rudimentary feeling that there is a journey and that you're part of it. And that's a little bit of wisdom which leads you to start to search. And in the searching behavior, you come across something—because it feels like it or is billed as having to do with it, you grab it and you work with it. And even sometimes, when it doesn't feel right, you keep doing it because you think you're supposed to keep doing it, because everybody else is doing it and because you can't quite agree that it isn't doing the thing you wanted it to, you know. We all get into those places.

And you learn, after a while, all you can do is be totally honest with yourself as to whether something's working or not. And when it's not, be honest enough to admit it's not working, and keep looking for something else.

Sometimes, when something isn't working, you know it's really working but you're resisting it and you may decide to stay in it even though it's hell. I do that oftentimes. So there's no clear rule that you drop it because it doesn't work. You have to trust your heart as to whether to stay in it or leave it at that point, okay?

Now, for some people, the major work they have to do is to open their heart. For others it's to quiet their mind. For others it's to come into their bodies more. You've got to listen and to hear better what you need to do.

Meditation

Quieting your mind is a good thing to begin doing, that is, pulling yourself in behind your attachment to body. That's what the meditative stance is about, and that's what meditation is about. So I think meditation is always a good place to start. Right? And I do just very simple meditations, not complex visualizations. I just meditate on my breath, just the in and out of the breath, that's all. I just do very simple things.

WOMAN: When you say "get behind the thought," what does that mean?

RAM DASS: As an example, if you do a one-pointed meditation, you start to follow your breath in and out. You've chosen a thought to attend to, which is the thought of breath, in and out. Then a thought will come, like, "This is never gonna work"—okay? (*Laughter.*) Now, at that point you've got a choice: you can either go with that thought or not. You can say, "Well,

I don't know if it'll work or not; after all, I have theoretical reason to believe it will," you know? The thought took you then; it threw out its little hook and it caught you and it's got you into a new place. Or you can say, "Look, I know you. You're a thought. Go sit down, have tea, I'm busy," and go back to following your breath. See?

And then, as you're following your breath, pretty soon another thought will come along, like "My knee hurts," or "I'm hungry," or whatever your thought is, you know. And it gets to the point where the thoughts will get more and more seductive. Like one thought will be "It's really happening!" You get a little rush in your spine or something and you think, "It's really happening!" That one usually really takes you, you know. (*Laughter.*)

But if you can get so you can just treat that as another thought, you let that one go, you just keep coming back, you keep coming back until pretty soon you're watching your thoughts go by. They're all coming, but they don't have the pull anymore because the attachment to the primary thought is strong enough—not through will, but just through the commitment to getting on with it, really. It's that one desire is stronger than the other desires. Like if your leg hurts, so it hurts because you're doing this other thing. You're not so busy making yourself feel good. Right? It's a hierarchy of desires, and you can only do it at the rate you can do it.

But you get so that you're watching your thoughts go by. All right? And then you're still with one thought, using that one thought to watch the other thoughts. And then, later, that one thought falls away. And then you go into other planes. But this is the stage you asked me about. This is what I meant by watching thoughts or getting behind thought.

IV. DYING

Before I take more questions, I'd like to deal with the dying thing just a little bit if I could because we're running behind time and I dig on that one. (*Very long pause.*) From a series of events that occurred in a period of about six or eight years, I found myself feeling differently about death than I had before.

Some of these things were the result of psychedelics. In the world of psychedelia, you keep going in and out of other planes of consciousness. And at first, if you do it very rarely, you go into a plane and you come back. And you do as Carl Jung said in *Memories, Dreams, Reflections*: "I came back finally to my family and reality." See? Because Jung always kept one place as "real" and all the rest of it was "fascinating," because he didn't want to give up being Carl Jung, right?

Ah, but if you keep doing it, if you say, "Damn the consequences," and keep going, if you open Pandora's box and give up trying to keep one foot in the door, you get to the point where all these other realities start to have the same validity as the one you're coming back to.

And it's not even clear that you're coming back; you're just going in and out of planes, and they're *all* another plane. "Reality" is just another plane, and even this one—the one in which we think we're meeting in a room at Esalen at this moment—becomes relative reality rather than absolute reality. Who you thought you were on this plane isn't who you experience being on other planes, and the question of what it is that's dying gets kind of interesting.

Then the next thing that fed into me was my relation with Aldous Huxley. Aldous and I had talked a lot about dying. He was dying of cancer at the time. He wrote *Island*, which describes a blueprint for a death, and which turns out to be the way he did his own death. He took LSD at the last. Laura gave him LSD, and they sat together and he described what was happening as he watched the body go. She said it was just a very peaceful thing where he was letting go quietly and just let go and went out. There was no holding, no clinging, right?

The next event in my series was my mother's death. I sat with her in the hospital, and I was on drugs most of the time, as was she. But we were on different drugs (*laughter*), and I saw that this body was dying, but I didn't see her dying. There was no doubt from where I was looking, through my mescaline-glazed or -clarified eyes, that something was dying, but it didn't seem to be my mother.

And it got to the point where she and I started to talk about it. She asked me what I thought death was, and I was the only one she could talk to because I seemed to be right there. Everybody else was into the hysterical denial trip, which most people are in hospitals. And I was awed from my own drug state about the horror of the hospital in terms of the total denial of the scene for everybody.

The next event in my series is my trip to India. I am in a Land Rover, very pukka, with a very wealthy guy, and I'm scared shitless of India, because it's so basic. (*Chuckles.*) It's too basic for a good middle-class Jewish boy from Boston. Right? And I'm in a Land Rover with taped Vivaldi concertos and canned salmon, and I'm looking out the window at India and taking slides through the window and I don't want to get too close because you get dysentery if you even look at anything, you know? (*Laughter.*)

So we come to Benares, which is the city of dying in India. It's the very sacred city where they have the burning ghats—where they've been burning bodies all day long and all night long for hundreds and thousands of years, literally. The bodies are burned and then thrown into the Ganges. I go out on the street one night by myself, and on the street are all these people with leprous sores. Their bones are this big around, and they're just dying. They've got these little begging bowls and they wear loincloths and they're all shriveled and dying and there's hundreds of them, and they look at you with wide eyes, you know, and they're holding out their bowls. The pull on me was so horrendous and the fact that I had a traveler's check in my pocket didn't help, you know. Here I was, a big healthy being, and these people were just dragging around. It was like being in a hell for me, it was just so horrible. I couldn't stand it. I just couldn't stand it. Pity was just overwhelming me. And I went back to the hotel room and literally hid out. I didn't want to go out because I couldn't stand it.

Six months later, I came back to Benares and I looked and walked through the streets. And I suddenly saw—to my absolute disbelief, at first, and then awe—that I had been looking at it from my egocentric predicament as a Westerner. Once I understood what Benares was and who these people were and what was happening, I realized to my astonishment that they were looking at *me* with pity. And all the time I'd been looking at *them* with pity.

Because, in fact, the greatest thing that can happen to a Hindu is that you can die in Benares. It's like only the very select few ever get to die in Benares, and these people were going to make it. See? And they were right—it's just like they were all in the moment before utter orgasm, and I'm going around feeling sorry for them. You know, they're in the ultimate place and there it's all right. I mean, it's all all right from where they're doing it. Because when they die, Shiva whispers in their ear the name of God and they become fully enlightened. That's the way that game works. See? And they know that, but I didn't know it.

So, from my point of view, I was busy with their bodies; *they* weren't busy with their bodies. They were just waiting to be rid of the damn bodies. From my old point of view, I wanted to hold on to my body, so it looked horrible to me, right? But their trip was very powerful in terms of my new perceptual state. Because then I looked at them and I saw that look; I mean, I was now looking from a new perceptual vantage place, and I saw a different thing looking back at me. Okay?

QUESTION: What about the children?

RAM DASS: Well, wait a minute, let's take one thing at a time. Let me work this one through, because we can't go on much longer and I'd rather deal with the whole dying thing first. I can handle that within karma and all, but, uh . . .

QUESTIONER: Okay.

RAM DASS: Ramonmaharishi was dying of cancer of the arm, and he had powers of healing. He had healed many people. They said to him, "Oh, heal yourself." He said, "No, this body's all used up." They started to cry and they wailed, "Don't leave us." Then he said, with astonishment, "Don't do this. Don't be silly, where could I go?" Like, if you think I'm going anywhere, that's your problem. I'm not going anywhere. I'm here; I'm just dropping a body.

It's like you're going to sell your Ford and somebody comes up to you and says, "Don't leave me, don't leave me." You say, "I'm not leaving you; I'm just selling the Ford." I mean that's the level at which he was. He was perplexed because, from his point of view, he wasn't going anywhere. It's like the Zen statement—

your coming and going is nowhere but where you are. And when you are here, you're here. And there's just coming and going. But you're still here.

Maharaji and Dying

Maharaji did a number of things that were very unusual about dying. Like one day he was walking with an old devotee, and he looked up in the sky and he said, "Ma so-and-so—an old woman follower of his—just died in this other city a couple of hundred miles away." He saw that with his mind. And she had, in fact, died. And he laughed and laughed and laughed. And the old devotee was very loyal and friendly, and he said, "Maharaji, you're a butcher! What're you laughing at, if she just died?" And Maharaji said, "Would you prefer that I made believe that I was one of the puppets? Would you like me to make believe that it's horrible when somebody dies? Would you like me to make believe that I should be sorry about it? Is that what you want me to do? Do you want me to play a part like I'm in the illusion? Is that what you want? Huh?"

Maharaji's sitting in this group of people, and suddenly he looks up and he says, "Who's here?" There's somebody here." "No, no, Maharaji, nobody new has come." And just then a man comes in and Maharaji looks at him and he says, "I know he's dying and I know he's suffering, but tell him I'm not coming." And the guy comes up and says, "Maharaji, how did you know? The man just had a heart attack, and I rushed over because he said, 'Go get Maharaji.' You must come, Maharaji." Maharaji says, "Nobody thinks I know anything. But I'm not coming." "Oh, Maharaji, you must come." "No. Here, give him this banana. Then he'll be all right."

Well, in India, when you give somebody a piece of fruit, it can be just a piece of fruit or it can be very special. Like I watched a couple come who were married for twenty-five years and they'd had no children, and they said, "Oh, Maharaji, please let us have a child before we die. We want a child." Maharaji said, "Here, here's a mango, for the husband." And nine months later, the wife has a baby. Everybody in India knows those things happen.

So the guy goes rushing to the man who is dying, with the banana, and they mash it up and they give it to the guy and he eats the whole banana and dies. Okay? Maharaji said he'd be all right after he ate the banana. He didn't say *how* he'd be all right. He's looking at it from a different place—about what all rightness is. Okay?

Working with People Who Are Dying

Well, I saw his teachings of this kind. Just being around a person for whom the dying thing meant something entirely different, plus my own experiences, plus my psychedelic experiences, plus what was starting to happen to me with meditation—where I was going in and out of my body and my social identity and whatever it is that seems to die—put me into a different feeling about it all. And when I came back to America, I started to look for opportunities to be with people who were dying.

This gal, Ginny, was an old associate of Ernest Hemingway's. She was out of that genre, a sort of liberal, intellectual, hip—a beautiful woman. And she had lived with the Huxleys for maybe twenty years. She was dying of cancer of the nervous system. And Laura Huxley called me and asked me if I would come and be with her. So I came to California and I went to see Ginny.

The first time I went, she was still pretty much her usual, very cynical, tough, intellectual, wonderful self—not a mystic, by any means. And I gave her all my words, and they all sounded like bullshit as I was saying them because she was hearing them and debating them and saying she couldn't believe them. We were talking about death. And I thought, well, I'm of no use to her at all.

And then, a few weeks later, she was near the end and Laura called me and I came back again. And this time Ginny was very weak and in very great pain through her lower stomach and her groin and thighs. She was writhing with pain. There was this (*makes a sharp, gasping sound*) kind of place. And I came into the room and I sat down next to her bed and I started to meditate, but instead of going away in my meditation, I stayed right here and I did the Buddhist Cemetery Meditation, which is a meditation on the decaying body. You stay right with it; you just use the stuff.

I just watched the process go on; I was just sitting quietly watching instead of judging it or getting freaked by the pain. I was just allowing it all, giving it space to be. I was letting God's design manifest without getting into a judgment of how I thought it ought to be, right? You understand? And I sat there and I got very quiet inside, very, very quiet, watching this process going on in her, watching the pain and the suffering and the decay and the dying. And she's all the time going through this writhing thing, and then she turns to me and she says, "I feel so very peaceful."

And at that moment, she and I entered into a profound space—so profound that the fact that we were in Los Angeles, the fact that we were on this planet, was irrelevant. From my space the room was luminous with light, and we were both sitting blissed out. The pain was going on—right?—and there was somebody reacting, but she wasn't it. Okay?

My vibration, my meditative space, had created an environment which would resonate with the place within her that was deeper than the place that was the experience of the pain. All right? And all I did was meditate. Right? I didn't do any mystical thing. All I did was quiet myself and not get into reacting to somebody dying—in other words, not get lost in the plane at which dying is occurring.

Zen Monks at Mount Sinai Hospital

Now, a friend of mine was telling me about her friend Debby. Debby is from a wealthy family, and she was dying in the pavilion of Mount Sinai Hospital. She was part of the Zen scene, the New York Zen scene. And all the Zen students decided to meditate in her private room at Mount Sinai Hospital every day instead of at the zendo. So they would come in and they'd meditate, right?

And the residents on the ward would be making rounds, see? And they'd come along with that pushing-open-the-door and the cheery "Well, how're we doing tonight?" You know. The hospital is a temple to the living, and the worst failure is a death; and so the whole thing is a denial of death because of everybody's panic about it. Well, the residents walk in and there's all these Zen monks sitting there and it freaks them completely. They don't know how to deal with it. And each night they're coming in a little more gently until finally they're like coming into a temple, you know, they're just honoring. And they're creating a space, so that when Debby died on Christmas Eve, it's just a release, a letting go—just a free letting go.

The Wild Strawberry Story

I want to tell you about a young man I know who is dying. The kid is a young hippie, and he's twenty-three and he's got Hodgkin's disease. A friend of mine, Wavy Gravy, asked me to talk to him. And I must preface this by saying that I had just been in a depression for a few weeks. And I had been just sitting, taking baths, reading novels, going to movies, and being depressed. Right? I allow myself all kinds of luxuries. I mean, I don't see any reason for not being depressed, you know. It's as interesting as anything else.

Okay. So Wavy Gravy asks me to talk with the kid. And I'm supposed to be a holy man, only I'm depressed. (*Laughter.*) So I meet him and I say, "I hear you're going to die soon." He says, "Yeah." Now, that's for openers, okay? And most people wouldn't play it that way. But what I'm saying is, from where I'm sitting what is dying isn't who we are. See? That's a reality for me. I'm looking at a place in you and I'm looking at a place in myself that isn't in time and space. And so, from where I'm looking, the kid is involved in a process which is a lot like puberty.

I notice he goes to light a cigarette and he's shaking as he lights it. So, I think, "Oh, wow, I'm screwing up the scene. And, you know, I went through my whole paranoid trip. So I said to him, "Hey, man, I don't mean to bug you. I mean, you're the one who's dying. You do it your way, and I'll leave you alone because I see you're nervous talking to me. I'm into doing good and . . . forget it, you know."

He said, "Well, I am nervous, but the reason I'm nervous is because I've been looking for the strength to die and you are the first person who's come along that isn't freaked by the predicament I'm in. I'm nervous because I can make a contact; I can get the thing I need. And I'm shaking because I'm so excited by what's happening at this moment." Right? He gave me the license at that moment, see?

He was planning to die by o.d.'ing on heroin and taking LSD. He was a street person, right? That seemed like as reasonable a way to die as any other way. And he was programming his own death; and I think a person should be free to program his own death. I'm not into judging how you should die.

At one point, we decided to go for a ride. We stopped for some gas and he said, "Could I drive? It'll probably be the last time I drive because I'm getting so weak." We were just talking about how he planned to die and working and being together. And so he started to drive. I said, "Sure, of course." That's a terribly romantic image, you know. A twenty-three-year-old asking, "Can I drive for the last time?"

He starts to drive and I suddenly realize he's too weak to turn the steering wheel, see? We're only going about twenty, but every time we come around a curve, we're aiming for the edge and I have to reach over and turn the wheel and I'm trying to do it like nothing's happening, you know? (*Laughter.*)

And I suddenly realize what's happening, that I'm getting caught in a conspiracy with him to make believe he is who he used to be because he can't live in the moment. And I said to him, "You realize what's happening? You and I are caught in a conspiracy, here, to protect an ego place that you're not wanting to give up. Why don't you just let go of all that stuff? You're too weak to drive, and you should be lying back and I should be driving. Let's just get into the present moment; let's stop trying to cling to the past. The present is this."

It's the wild strawberry story, you know. As you're going off the edge of the cliff, there's the strawberry and how sweet it tastes, and the hell with the tigers above and below—it's always the moment of the strawberry. And the strawberry is in this: in being with the present moment, not in yesterday or tomorrow.

And I learned a lot from him about how to keep it right here (*snaps fingers*), because I realized then that the best preparation for dying was in living each moment in the present. From all the Eastern literature and the way I understand it, the game is to stay fully conscious at the moment of death—so that, as you're dying, you're right here, and as the body goes, you're right here, and it's just a continuum of consciousness even though the body falls off. Otherwise you can get caught in the pain or the melodrama of the fear of ceasing to be who you thought you were, which is what it turns out to be to die.

A Center for Dying

What this has led me to is an attempt to create, or to conceive of, or to talk about, a metaphor for dying in America—an attempt to create a new space for people to die in. To be quite honest, I have only been interested in people who seek to die consciously. I am not interested in the general population, because everybody dies and most people's karma is such that they are not ready to awaken in this lifetime or maybe for many more yet.

So I am interested in creating a model environment with optimum conditions for people who ask to die consciously with as much or as little medical help as they want. They couldn't have a doctor to kill them, but he couldn't keep them alive if they didn't want to stay alive. We did this with Ginny. Ginny and Laura and I would discuss each decision about intravenous feeding and stuff like that. She had a say in what she wanted. It was her body.

They could die in whatever religious metaphor they wanted, but in addition they would have a guide. Okay? They would have a guide; they would have somebody with them who was working. The guide is not a professional "dier," because who's a professional "dier"? The guide is somebody who is working on himself through working with somebody who is dying.

A doctoral dissertation has just been done which, as many doctoral dissertations do, demonstrated the obvious scientifically. And in this case the demonstration is that people who have taken psychedelics or people who have been meditating for three years or longer are significantly different from the general population in their anxiety about death. All right? We all knew that, but it's nice to know it, you know? The author of that dissertation is Charlie Garfield, and he and I have become partners in this work.

My Own Death

Once a year, I take acid. I may never do it again, so I shouldn't state it as a law. I have thus far started taking acid once a year. What I usually do is, I go out in the desert and I fast for a while and I take acid. But this one time, two years ago, I found myself taking it in Salina, Kansas, (*laughter*) because that's where I happened to be when it came time to take acid.

I'm alone, I'm feeling peace, I'm in a cool place, and my mind turns toward God. These are the conditions in which acid can be useful in a limited way, according to my guru. I set up the room. I've got Maharaji's picture on the television set, and the television set's on, but the volume is off, so all these images are coming out of his head. And I've got candles and incense on the set. I've even got these Tibetan tankas I'm carrying in the trunk of my car for somebody, and I set them up all over the room. Room 125 has turned into a very beautiful place, and I'm naked and I've taken a bath and I've taken acid.

Now, I start to get higher than I thought I was going to get and I freak and I think, "What has been done to me? Is someone getting back at me somehow?" you know? And I get a whole grade-B paranoid movie going, which is familiar to many people. (*Laughter.*)

I want to run. I have an impulse to run out and get the motel manager, and I remember I'm naked. I wonder, "What am I going to do?" So I *think* (*laughter*) and I imagine the motel manager, and from his point of view, I see this naked, bearded, bald man from Room 125. He'll call the police, and I can see the hospitals and the Thorazine and the whole trip. (*Laughter.*) And it probably leads to my death one way or another.

I pull back from the door, and I think, "Well, maybe I can think of another way, other than going to get help, so that I won't have to die." See? So I fall down and I go through a number of trips in which every way I think of to go through, to not die, turns out to lead to my death anyway. Some of them take forty years, but I'm going to die anyway, because it's inevitable that whoever I think I am is going to die. No matter who I keep thinking I am, that one's going to die too, see?

I finally see my predicament: as long as I keep thinking I'm anybody, I'm going to die. And I finally say to Maharaji, "Okay, I'm ready; let me die. I want to die. I want to give up." And at that moment, I lay down and say, "Okay." And then there is (*makes a snapping sound*) a gap; the next thought I have is, "Wow, now I can be anybody I want to be."

Now, that gap may have lasted a millionth of a second or it may have lasted a long time—who knows? I wasn't keeping time. But the fact is that at that time my karma was such that I had to be reborn immediately, if you will, back in the thought. At that point I might have just stayed. Some beings stay at that point. But I came right back because there was still stuff to be done; I could feel that happening, okay?

But I felt, in a sense, a certain sense, a kind of freedom. And I knew that, as I got back into being who I now would be, that I would again start to get subtly attached to my thought forms of who I was, and that when the next time came to die I was still going to suffer again. And I was going to keep suffering as long as I had any attachment to the thought forms of who I was being. Okay? But I saw that the suffering was only because of my identity with the thought forms, and that each time the thought form was going to die. And I would keep being born and dying as long as I was attached to thought forms.

I really feel now, on a much deeper experiential level, that all that dies is the thought of who we are. Right?

PART TWO

Gestalt Awareness Strategies in the Training of People-Helpers

John B. Enright, Ph.D.

I was for three and one-half years a nonresident member of Synanon, a "self-help" group founded by an ex-drunk, Charles E. Dederich, which, along with many other activities, has provided a setting in which hundreds of heroin users have successfully cleaned up. It has also provided an exciting encounter community for thousands of ordinary citizens. In Synanon I was exposed to several figure-ground reversals that have taught me some crucially important lessons not usually available to members of the helping professions. The lesson relevant here is that ordinary people have a natural inclination and a great capacity to be helpful to their fellow men. When this capacity is systematically fostered, many quite ordinary people—and some who seem at first glance to be quite deeply disturbed—can develop a skill in helping others that would be unbelievable to most professionals, who seem to cling

This paper was presented in a symposium on Gestalt Awareness Training for Mental Health Professionals and Paraprofessionals at the American Psychological Association convention in Hawaii, September 1972.

(for socioeconomically understandable reasons) to the conviction that professionals have some kind of monopoly on helping skills.

People learn to be good and effective human beings from other human beings whom they admire and look up to. This process of voluntarily modeling oneself after another is a crucial part of becoming a human being, and most disturbances in living can be seen as reflecting a lack or distortion of such learning. Frequently, in my training groups, I ask participants to submit a dozen or so incidents in which they were significantly helped by another human being. In a definite majority of the incidents submitted, the "help" was completely unintentional and unconsciously done. The other person was simply "doing his thing" in a visible, available way, and the "helpee" took what he wanted and learned what he needed to learn. Incidents of conscious, intentional helping were less frequently reported. Apparently, in any human community, there is a sprinkling of people who, by simply being there in a solid, ethical, effective, and available way, act as invisible "helpers" to many others in the community. The occasional acts of overt conscious helping they engage in are like the tip of the proverbial iceberg. The people who do this kind of "helping" must not only have qualities worth learning, but have them available; hence openness and free self-disclosures are necessary attributes of these natural, spontaneous "helpers."

The foregoing point of view is based on my long Synanon experience, my exposure to other self-help groups after that, and the work and training I have been doing since then. Growing from this position is the conviction I now have that ordinary people with some of the qualities described above, augmented with some good training, can provide all the psychological help that is necessary for all but a tiny minority of people, including those people that have been caught up in a destructive and degrading definitional system by being called "patients." Rather than seeing such ordinary people as substitutes for professionals, I find it interesting to view professionals as substitutes for these empathic, open, and realistic "ordinary" people.

This is not to deny that various therapies can be helpful. Each therapeutic strategy—increasing insight, awareness, or understanding, desensitizing or reconditioning, dissolving body armor, and so on—can be helpful to certain people at certain times. The problem has been that these strategies are often applied *instead of* rather than *in addition to* the more basic process of human helping described above. In the process of learning his skill the expert professional has too often become too removed and unavailable *as a human being* to his client. Therapy done from the expert role is a little like walking up the down escalator: losing ground in one way while gaining in another. Many therapists are quite explicit about being detached experts, unavailable for role modeling (in which case, of course, they are providing role models of detachment and unavailability). Others, recognizing the importance of modeling, try to combine the expert role with modeling; but the apparent safety and invulnerability of the professional-expert role make it a very subtly enticing one, very hard to disengage from completely.

In the last few paragraphs, I have tried to create a figure-ground reversal that I now wish to make explicit. Since I believe that *people* are the natural agents for helping people and can do it, I refuse to look on people as "paraprofessionals." Rather, in their distancing quest for the safe "expert" role, the professionals have frequently become "parapeople." In this essay, I will concentrate on the use of Gestalt methods in training people, leaving the training of "parapeople" to my colleagues. My goal in training people is not to make them quasi-, pseudo-, or para-professionals, but to develop the basic model of good, effective, self-disclosing human beings. In this endeavor, some of the skill and knowledge of the "expert" disciplines is useful, if it can be used without introducing the dangerous side effects of the expert model. Specifically, some of the strategies of Gestalt Awareness Training have been particularly adaptable and I will focus on them.

Up to now, I have used Gestalt training methods with several hundred people, including Awareness House counselors, "rap center" volunteers, ministers, probation officers, police officers, high school counselors and teachers, women's discussion-group leaders, and many others. Many are, or are in a position to become, the kind of key community people I described earlier. Some are in explicitly "helping" roles, others not. They are *not* fully trained Gestalt therapists ("mini-Fritzes"). Though they are not therapists, if enough of them were around doing their thing I suspect the number of people "needing therapy" might be decreased markedly. In most training situations Gestalt has not been the only mode of training. I have varied the amount of time spent on Gestalt from ten to close to one hundred hours. In the format I am developing now, explicitly Gestalt training occupies about twenty-five of sixty hours. The rest of the time is spent in learning such things as active listening, self-disclosure, and some encounter techniques, and a personal life review and work with contracts and ethics.

Having taken half of my time to describe who I am training and for what, and the context in which the Gestalt training takes place, I will now get on to the specific strategies I have found useful, first describing some of the techniques concretely, then summarizing what they are designed to convey.

The Continuum of Awareness

Working in subgroups of three or four, I have people, one at a time without interruption, begin a series of sentences with the phrase "Now I am aware" and finish it with whatever is salient in their awareness at that moment. If their dominant awareness is something they prefer not to say, I ask them to report the awareness of censoring. Several phenomena usually emerge from this experiment and are discussed. Great individual differences are usually noted and commented on; some people are almost exclusively aware of external phenomena, some are mostly in their memories or in anticipation or speculating about others, while still others report mostly internal sensations. Usually everyone notices (in others, of course) extensive gaps between reported awareness and ongoing behavior of obvious importance.

There are several variations of this procedure. One, the "observe-imagine" game, breaks the root verb *aware* into two components: awareness of something sensorily present at the moment of awareness (observation, or noticing) and everything else (for which I suggest the verb "imagine"). For example, a frequent report in the first experiment might be "I am aware you are bored with what I am saying." In the new format, this becomes, for example, "I notice you yawning and looking away; I imagine you are bored." This experiment begins to call attention to the incessant process of assuming and speculating—imagining I can "know" what another person is experiencing.

A second variation focuses on the fact that some

contents of awareness seem to be selected actively, others being "given" without any feeling of choice. This usually leads to some experiments on deliberate censoring, demonstrating that genuine freedom to censor freely usually leads to greater openness.

Almost always, we also work with the process of organismic evaluation. The myth of neutral, objective perception is deeply rooted in our culture and needs to be exposed. Returning to the basic awareness exercise, the person is asked to add after each awareness the phrase "and I find it pleasant" or "and I find it unpleasant." At first, this often feels forced, but it becomes quite easy. At times, we also work with the judging process ("and I judge it good" or "and I judge it bad"). Frequently, there is some poignant humor as we run experientially into awareness that is found pleasant and judged bad or found unpleasant and judged good. Our culture produces entirely too many of these!

Body Awareness

The second group of experiments drawn from Gestalt training focuses on body experience as the locus of organismic meaning. The most dramatic starting point is the face. I have people close their eyes and concentrate on feeling their face from inside, noticing loci of tension without relaxing. After a few seconds I suggest they gradually intensify whatever tension is there, to augment whatever expression is there, adding as little new as possible. As the face becomes more tense in some way, I suggest that they stay open to noticing other parts of the body, to see if anything else tenses up, and also note if any thoughts, images, or memories occur. As the expressions become more extreme, I suggest that they find some words or phrases that convey what is being expressed, whether it is new or familiar.

This experiment usually demonstrates quite dramatically for some people that the body is carrying memories and feelings of a surprisingly strong and clear nature, accessible to deliberate attention, though quite out of awareness without such attention. (It is not infrequent for memories several years old, or even long-ignored childhood memories, to be reintegrated in this experiment, though it is equally likely to be a leftover feeling from earlier in the day that emerges.) For many the most important discovery in this experiment is that rich, complex psychological meaning emerges simply from keeping attention directed steadily on somatic sensations. Often this is the clearest demonstration of the decisive superiority of simple experiencing over concept manipulation in the search for personal meaning.

Another approach to the body is to ask people to freeze completely at some signal and, during the period of time they remain unmoving, to notice all postural tensions and how all parts of the body are related to each other and to the environment. During this experiment I may ask people to find some point of tension and develop a dialogue between the two parts involved. (Head: "Thanks, arm, for holding me up." Arm: "You're welcome, but you are getting a little heavy—I wish you'd carry your own weight for a while." Head: "No, it's right that you should take care of me; I'm pretty important and necessary to you.") At times these dialogues lead to obvious analogues to ongoing interpersonal relationships. An interesting variation is to have one person freeze and everyone else copy his posture as precisely as possible. In their reports of their experience in this "borrowed" posture, the copiers learn an approach to physical empathy in understanding another, while the originator of the posture learns some things he has become too habituated to notice directly in himself. We usually do six to ten of these body experiments, and participants often make considerable progress in learning their own gesture-posture language.

Projection and Identification

The third group of experiments begins by going in the opposite direction: outward. I ask people to let their eyes wander around the room and pick some object that stands out for them. ("Let it pick you," I often say.) Then I ask them to *be* that object: make statements of any kind, as though their center of consciousness were that object. For example, as one of the ceiling beams, a woman said, "I'm very old-fashioned and uselessly ornate. I have a heavy load to bear, and I'm not getting much help; the nearest other beam is a long way away." Each person works by himself for a few minutes. I feed in a few suggestions as they work, particularly suggesting that, when they feel like stopping, they get back into the object and say a few more things. Usually the point of stopping is just when a person is approaching some more involving content. I suggest that they make one or two statements about what they are definitely *not* as the object. Sometimes I will wave my magic wand and allow them to make one change in themselves as the object. After a few minutes, those who feel like it share what they discovered and continue the process out loud. Though each experiment in the whole series is chosen by a few as the most useful, this particular one is most frequently felt to be the most powerful and dramatic, leading as it does with unbelievable directness to current core concerns. It is a very startling experience to watch someone with obvious feeling and sincerity respond to facets of an object very different from those to which I respond. I am sitting there knowing absolutely what is salient and important about this object, and he is sitting there sincerely knowing something very different. People generally seem to act on an assumption that, if verbalized, would be something like this: "If others don't agree with me, it is just that they don't see things as clearly as I." This experiment, among other things, provides a powerful challenge to that unexplicated belief.

Several related experiments follow this one. If the group seems ready and we have time, we go on to dreams, using dream images as starting points. Finally, I have people select someone who is very troublesome for them and practice consciously projecting on that person.

Interactional Habits

Most of the experiments up to this point have been essentially individual, with each person working on himself. Identification, empathy, and learning from each other have been frequent, but there has been little interaction. This is deliberate; most human interaction is so heavily laced with projection that it is more apparent than real, with each person reacting more to his concept of the other than to the actual other. Having laid the groundwork by such exercises as the observe-imagine game and projection, we are readier to confront the difficulties of interaction. (One of my favorite images is to say that staying centered, aware, and responsible in a group is like flying a kite in a whirlwind.)

The last set of exercises focuses on *style* or *form* of interaction rather than content. Instructions for the first experiment are simple. In groups of six to eight, participants are asked to talk about anything they want in any way, with one limitation: ask no questions. Confine all verbalisms to *statements*. I participate actively, role-modeling the process, pointing out questions, helping rephrase them, and so on. Within forty-five minutes to an hour, the results of this experiment are clear. Truly necessary and unmanipulative questions are so rare as to be almost nonexistent. During this time, many participants discover quite clearly their own particular manipulative use of questions—to avoid risk, trap others, play helpless and get others to do their work for them, show off, and so forth.

The next style change is to ask people to eschew all impersonal and indirect forms of speech ("one," the impersonal "you," "it," "we," "people," for example) and confine themselves to *I* messages. All I know for sure is what *I* think, see, feel, and so on. Saying it any other way is an attempt to shuck responsibility and clarity. Many people report considerable anxiety as they come out from behind their impersonal speech, but also more clarity and energy. A frequent comment participants make is that in this mode of talk, talking is harder, but listening is easier.

The most difficult style change to pinpoint, but the most crucial, is speculation about others. The classic format is "I think that you think. . . ." All sentences starting that way are forbidden, and people are asked to report *only their experience*, not the conclusions they draw about others' experiences. "My "perception" that "you are bored" can always, with close attention, be traced back to some feeling in *me*: my own boredom or irritation, or perhaps the uneasy feeling I have that I am not worth listening to. Some people, especially analytically oriented therapists, are almost paralyzed by this game. They have focused on others so long that they are almost completely unable to find *their own direct experience* that underlies their speculation (whether right or wrong). This is probably the most difficult experiment of the whole series and works as well as it does only because of the hours of groundwork laid by the previous experiments.

About four or five hours' work with these three experiments is not enough to lead to permanent change, but for most participants it gives a clear feeling of how muddy and obstructive impersonal, speculative, questioning speech is and some concrete notion of what to do about it.

There are three "themes," or principles, that run through all the above experiments; each game is a different approach to one or more of these principles. Probably, any one experiment done in sufficient depth would teach all that can be taught; the variety simply makes the process easier and catches more people where they happen to be ready to hear.

1. The way to know myself is to attend to my *experience*, not to my *concepts about* my experience. If I simply attend to what is happening in me, concentrating on *what* is happening rather than standing back from it speculating and why-ing, then all I need to know will flow directly out of that experience. Once I learn the truth of this for myself, it is relatively easy to apply it to others.

2. All I am ever really in touch with is myself. All I "know" about another is mediated through myself. I cannot perceive in another anything that is not, in germ at least, existent in me at that moment, and my opinion about what is important to another is heavily influenced by what is important to me. The constant return to this theme teaches a kind of humility and recognition of the constant danger of "laying my trip" on another whenever I get interested and involved.

3. I am totally responsible for my experience. I

am the "cause" of all that happens to me, and you are for you. Rather than saying to a client, "You need help," I recognize that I have a need to help at that moment, and he is the most convenient target. This clear owning of my own feelings and needs—and the clear assignment to others of *their* feelings and needs—releases me from helping games, whether initiated by me or the client, and opens up the possibility of genuine human help.

To me it seems clear that if A and B are interacting, and A is living consistently with these three principles, then B is very likely to gain from the relationship. If I know how to know myself and others, can distinguish what is me from what is the other, and take full responsibility for myself, it hardly matters if I am intentionally "helping" someone or just skipping rocks with him. If I am intentionally helping, it hardly matters what "method" I am using or whether I am a person or "paraperson"; some help is likely to happen.

One View of Gestalt Therapy: An Evening Discussion with Trainees

Stephen Schoen, M.D.

I became a Gestalt therapist in the past five years, after eight years in practice as a self-styled existential therapist, because I wanted to develop myself further as the best possible therapist I could be—not with the intent of being a "Gestalt therapist" at all (note the quotation marks). Gestalt therapy can be an introject, like anything else, a foreign-body technique that I take in but don't assimilate. The most difficult lesson to learn in Gestalt training is to be free of the imitative, the technique teachable by rote from rules. Gestalt has two levels, the one "meta" to the other. The deeper, "meta" level says: "Be yourself. Honor what is in you and in others, unedited." The other, superficial, technical level offers the rules, ploys, and jargon which Fritz Perls, himself a therapeutic genius, developed, and which other therapists have modified, in order to increase awareness of personal truth. The difficulty is that the techniques in themselves are so potent, like toy firecrackers that can start real explosions, and so fascinating, like the real explosions begun with toy fireworks. It's easy to be seduced by them and so to miss the deep way, the "true way"—no more facile, no less austere, in Gestalt than for Pilgrim in *Pilgrim's Progress.* Do I sound heavy? Perhaps, but as I see it, something very sober and disciplined is built into the warmth, the lightness, and the bursts of drama and revelation for which Gestalt is also noted.

I consider therapy a *learning experience.* In Gestalt, one learns what is basic to its rules: the presentness and personalness of awareness, life as excitement, responsibility for oneself, and above all, freedom and flexibility with oneself. Obviously, there is a host of assumptions in this view of human nature, from which I extrapolate three working principles: First, that something else is possible and happens. Second, that people are false to themselves, get rigid, get caught in a self-generated crush against themselves. Third, that if they could see a way to *learn,* to be truly free of this pressure, they would prefer to. The Gestalt therapy I practice offers to teach the way to freedom by guiding the person to reclaim his native manysidedness.

How, then, does the "learning" in therapy take place? True learning is not imitative, yet the Gestalt methods are powerful conditioning agents, able to instill powerful external patterns. Isn't there a tendency in these methods to model a person a particular way—for instance, to shape him as dramatic or acquisitive? My position as a therapist aiming at personality reclamation is this: what is learned is increasing ease and flexibility with oneself, learning something truly new, learning to open up. The dramatic, the acquisitive, and God knows what else may emerge; but, above all, the training is in preparedness for the unexpected. In Gestalt therapy we're like porpoises being taught to do something unexpected with ourselves, for the effective trainer is like a good therapist—both a supporter and a frustrater of old habits. He proceeds like this: First he trains the porpoise to a particular action—say, a sideward flip—by rewarding him with a fish each time he behaves correctly. Being bright, the porpoise learns the desired behavior after several training sessions. Then a time comes when he does the sideward flip and he does *not* get a fish. He repeats it, again no fish; again repeat, again no fish. He appears frustrated and angry, swims around in random behavior, and after a while, quite accidentally, does a forward flip, for which he is now rewarded. Training proceeds as before for this new behavior. When it is securely learned, it, too, is suddenly not rewarded. New frustration, anger, random movement, accidental backward flip—and reward. So matters go, through reinforced "accidental" learnings. So far this appears as behavioral reinforcing, conditioned behavior, until a time when the porpoise puts something together. And then, in the next training session, without warning, he executes, in a series, fifteen new and different flips, three of which have never been reported before in the species! He has learned a new concept, *flipping*, and moved to a new level.

The chief difference for human beings is that the therapist is, so to speak, another porpoise! And as such, beyond his authority with his patient, he is able to teach a role model; he exemplifies the reality of doing something all his own. In this way he is teaching his patient a new frame for all his experience. And the Gestalt model communicates several values: not only freedom with oneself but the warmth of the freedom, not only fearlessness but the sturdiness of living courageously.

I am a *philosophical* therapist. I "talk ideas" with my patients, as I've begun doing here with you. Opposing the conventional Gestalt opposition to "talking about," I want to make a pitch right now for the therapeutic value of ideas, of literature, and of words well chosen. We create our existence from our credos; we change our lives as our credos change. Gestalt therapy itself reaches people through its ideas and concepts, as well as through its emphasis on actual experiencing. And within therapy, joy, anger, grief, are experienced in a context of idea-laden behavior—in Gestalt groups the context of loving approval for freely feeling and expressing the grief or the joy. This idea may not be explicitly verbalized, but implicitly *is*: Take Fritz Perls's eloquent formula for encouraging awareness of self: describe one's actions through an ordinary day, prefacing each sentence with the words "This is my existence."

Fritz was a master of both language and nonverbal expression; grunts, howls, gibberish, also have unique value, as he demonstrated. But assuming, as many body therapies today seem to, that "words won't express how I feel" is, in my view, giving up a grand resource on which all culture is premised. Verbalization as true self-expression begins for us human beings at the age of two and assumes primacy over nonverbal, nonsymbolic vocalization in later life.

Currently some therapists are linking Gestalt therapy with certain unitary Oriental philosophies, setting as therapeutic goals getting beyond dualistic thought, beyond the distinction between subject and object. Now, the general understanding is that Gestalt psychology grew out of European existentialism, which assumes that my "self" is different from your "self," that there is a "self" and an "other." How can I appreciate you "in your uniqueness" if there isn't really this differentiation between subject and object?

To analyze this core question, let us go back to basic concepts. In European thought the subject-object split goes back to Descartes's division between "primary qualities" (such as extension and duration, which are *outside,* or *external to,* the person) and "secondary qualities" (like sensation, which is *within,* or *internal to,* the person). In Freud's thinking, this dichotomy was transferred whole in the notion of the libido "cathecting" objects, that is, concentrating its internal energy on external things and people as the way of forming bonds. An intrinsic alienation between *internal* self and *external* other is assumed.

The other view, that of a continuum of being throughout the world, is not only Oriental. It is the temper of mystical thought everywhere: of Blake's aphorism "One thought fills immensity"; of Plato's transcendent reality; of Tolstoy's affirmation, as a dying man of eighty, that "God is that infinite whole of which I am conscious of being a finite part." Within this view, alienation from wholeness is still possible. In Plato's cave I see others only as shadows. Exiled from Tolstoy's Christian Paradise, I suffer from the lack of God's grace. But in order to exist at all, the wholeness requires human relationship. As Martin Buber says, "I can face you, and indeed all the world, as my personal Thou." And by virtue of our interdependent *dual* existences, I am affirmed in my own existence.

To go beyond dualism, as I understand the word, doesn't imply the identity of everything. Differences exist but are connected, like a necklace connecting the beads on it—or shall we say, pearls? We shall! The pearls are separate one from another but are related to one another on the continuous thread. The existentialists talk about how each pearl must carry on its responsibility itself. The Orient, on the other hand, is interested in how the pearls are strung together, related to one another by the string, defined by it, and get a kind of energy from it. "Every being who has gone through the adventure of living *is* myself." This statement of the French novelist Marguerite Yourcenar refers to the thread, the uniting energy, the truth of communality, of having *experienced*—however different—the actual event. But also, without the real separations of one person and another, without *distancing*, as Buber has also said, you have no chance for *relationship*, for personal differentiation, ripening, commitment.

In the process of experiencing other people, you must differentiate between clear perception and projection. The one thing that saves you from projecting all over the place is "checking out" with the other person. My experience, even with quite psychotic people, is that when you "read" them in a way that is valid to them, you are focusing clearly. For instance, you may hear a disjointed, puzzling, breathless account; say to the client, "You sound upset," and the person very likely feels that an essential message of his has gotten across. In general, what clients want from you is that you communicate better with them than they at the moment are communicating with themselves. And the extraordinary thing—the daily miracle of communication—is that when you do that, they recognize it. It's as if you've held up a clear mirror. And they feel better both for the clarity and for the contact. When you just project, this doesn't happen. It's true that, in a folie-à-deux situation, you project and the other person, desperate to please you, will accept a view of himself that doesn't fit him. But when he is chiefly bent like this on pleasing you, he looks so anxious and so ungratified that you have plenty to warn you about what's going on.

QUESTION: I'm interested in your liking to talk ideas to patients. I associate Gestalt with attention to feelings, and ideas with traditional analytic work. How does your style connect with the patient's feelings? Do you place emphasis on feelings?

DR. SCHOEN: I'm glad you asked this. I wanted to come back to it. First of all, I place a hundred percent emphasis on working with people's feelings. That's where the interchange of the therapy is at! But I think you get on a dangerous spot if you assume there really is any separation between what a person feels and how he thinks about himself. The two are like two planes of the four-dimensional figure that we all are. Ideas, then, are just another way of getting to a person's feelings.

For instance, a girl says to a man who is in the room with her—this is during a conjoint session with me—"You lied to me about so-and-so." He replies, "You made me lie. I just couldn't do anything else, given all the things going on between us then." Well, that's the kind of statement that leads me to jump in with an idea. I discuss just what he means by the girl "making him" lie. He felt threatened by her under stress. That was a real provocation from "outside" him. And then he lied. Which takes us straight to a big point in Gestalt therapy: *responsibility*. How any of us comes on—whether we lie, tell the truth, stand on our heads, walk backwards, get anxious, or whatever—is really something which we ourselves originate. So he "had to" lie at the time. The lie is *his* doing, not hers, and in fact opens up interesting questions as to what behavior he decides on and what sense of alternatives he has.

Now this is the sort of idea-talk I'm likely to develop with patients, particularly if they're intellectual and interested in ideas, as this fellow is. But, to generalize, I'd say that all the directives which Gestaltists give patients *are* ideas. For instance, when I suggest to a person who fears that closeness will deprive him of independence, "Say to each person in the room, as you touch him or her and then move away, 'I can be close to you, and I can distance myself from you, *at will*,' " I offer him a new idea for experiencing himself.

One more point about experiencing as a *value*.

Another patient, aware of his slavish attachment to a girl and the violent anger he felt toward her as his captor, sighed to me, "I guess I still have to go through a lot of anger with her. I don't feel it right now, though, and I wish I didn't have to look forward to it." But, as I told him, he appreciated the karma of enslaving-dependence-leading-to-anger; and, since he did wish to be unenslaved, why assume that the anger must go on "over and over"? More idea-talk, you notice. "I *like* that," he answered, suddenly cheerful, as though the weather were much better than he could have expected. In fact, we *don't* have to experience every variety, say, of suffering, to get the Buddha's message: "The origin of suffering is desire." It's as though we were porpoises who could learn, after several surprisingly unrewarded back flips, that a back flip *and* a front flip *and* a side wiggle will *all* fail to get a fish from God.

I look upon the awareness of restrictive patterns as slides which we can move "out of the projector"—isn't that a happy metaphor?—without having to go through every feeling on the slide. We keep the slide "in our projector" as long as it looks good to us. Which, it's true, is often longer than we like to admit.

QUESTION: How do you personally "turn on" to your patients?

DR. SCHOEN: God knows, the turn-on is vital to me, for work that's successful or, at the least, interesting.

Well, in the first place, though I've been talking traditionally enough with you about "patients," I look on my patients not as such, but as persons I want to get to know. When I was first studying psychiatry, I was much influenced by Harry Stack Sullivan. I remember a talk by him that diagrammed the integrative relations between client and therapist during a first appointment. He drew lines between the two persons' "self-systems"

—that is, the relatively anxiety-free areas of both which established secure contact. My own homely version of his picture is this: I find all the ways that I "get with" the person, which lead me to feel, "Yes. I see. Very interesting. Yes, funny." Or "That's hard. I see, that's painful." Or "Yes, that's a drag." But when I wonder, "What's that? Say that again, please? I don't follow," and so on, my attention fastens on something that feels confused, that is obscurely fraught to me. And then it is up to me to be clear about what I want, clear on what bothers me about what bothers him. The game is up if I cannot make this convincingly important to him. Now, that is where Gestalt hijinks are dangerous. For the therapist to startle the patient, for instance, with "Pay attention to your left hand!" avails little if the patient is complaining about his right foot—*unless* the therapist is able to make plain to the patient his own sense of the connection.

For me, "turning on" to the patient means, quite literally, responding to his aliveness—the sense of being caught up in something growing, the spark of real give and take, as with a close friend or a lover. This happens only because I want it and the other person wants it.

There are people who don't seem interested in liveliness, and I can't work with them. I can be quite specific with you about my limits here; I've thought a good deal about them. I cannot work with people who want to control themselves better! Quite a few people want to, you know. Not many who call me; some god weeds them out before they phone. And I have nothing to offer them, since I'm not interested in anyone controlling himself better. I'm interested in people controlling themselves *less*. I think we take good care of ourselves when we're *not* putting constraints on ourselves. But these people—they go in psychiatric jargon as obsessive-compulsive types—want self-control. They want to be right, to be "clear," "to get it all straight." I have sawed back and forth on the log with them for weeks to months, trying with little or no success to ease their burden. Recently I've felt wiser, and I've been asking them to leave early in the game. The other people I do not work with are those who want to control others better. There are many such. They want to make conquests, sexual—well, territorial (they look on others really as territories), they want others at their feet. In psychiatric slang, they're called "psychopathic." And I can't go on with them because I don't want to help them to their goal, nor have them achieve it on me!

A typical question which both the self-control people and the conquest-oriented people ask me is "Can you give me an exercise to cope with this particular tension?"—a pain in the head or whatever. And in the way they ask, I don't hear any wish to express themselves more freely. The project of coping better is their goal. Well, I once did try very hard to help. I'd think, "Maybe I know an exercise. You can lie on the floor and breathe deep. You can breathe into the tension. Or you can have the tension speak. Or . . ." you know, the varied repertoire of Gestalt therapy and bioenergetics. Now I ask them why they want the exercise. And they get annoyed at me, and soon they are saying they want to manipulate other people better or to stop certain feelings from coming over them. And I reply that I don't think I have much to offer them. Then they're hurt; they feel misled. They had wanted a "Gestalt therapist," and I was supposed to be one. And then they go away, thank God! I believe I especially miss their lack of humor about themselves. I value a sense of humor highly, the willingness to play with one's usual way of carrying on in the world.

QUESTION: Do you do body work?

DR. SCHOEN: I'll give you an example. A fellow with

whom I've worked for a few months came in the other day complaining about knots in his stomach, and I wished to do something to help him feel better. Well, much of my work is verbal, but the body has its own language, which does concern me. So I had him lie on the floor on his back, breathe as freely as he could—by which I mean deep abdominal breathing, with loosened belt, no constraint around the middle. All of a sudden, he started to feel tearful, and I left his belly for his eyes. The tears began, but they would not flow. Then he had something to say: he felt he'd made an awful mistake in the last week. He had a long history of devastating alcoholism, loss of jobs and relationships, expensive hospitalizations. He'd been free of this for a long time, but he'd gotten into it again this week—that was his terrible mistake. He was over it now, but very shaky. Sitting beside him on the floor, I asked, "Can't you give yourself permission to make a mistake?" The question turned out to be very charged for him. He had a rush of thoughts about how he was never supposed to make a mistake as a child; his parents were perfectionistic with him, and he had continued to buy that in his adult life. It was mind-blowing to "give himself this permission." But he wanted to. And suddenly he was really crying: tears of release that were happy. Then I got back to his belly, suggesting he breathe into the knots, and he was nodding and crying and doing it. And the knots started to relax. And lo and behold! we got the best of both worlds: a deep assumption of his life was reexamined, with vast emotional liberation; and the stomach-knots that went with the assumption, but which were his only complaint at first, also loosened.

By the way, I make much these days of *giving oneself permission.* People seem to harbor at least *one* thing that isn't all right. Ninety-nine things out of a hundred about me are all right, but then there's that one! "I shouldn't run away from my problems," for instance. Why *shouldn't* you run away from your problems? I can't think of a better thing to run away from! You may come back refreshed and really solve something!

QUESTION: So you experiment with having people do the things that they don't allow themselves to do?

DR. SCHOEN: That's a good way to put it.

QUESTION: Can that cause trouble for patients who are, say, borderline psychotic and might get so involved with new feelings that they go "overboard"?

DR. SCHOEN: Borderline psychotic people don't give themselves permission to be sane! People who want to be crazy, you know, are assuming that sanity is a terrible price to have to pay, that the only sense and comfort lie in craziness. Since I think that sanity is great, full of adventures and rewards, I push it.

QUESTION: What do you mean by "sanity"?

DR. SCHOEN: I like Sullivan's phrase: what can be "consensually validated." If I hear the voice, you should be able to hear it too—unless you're deaf, and then we can agree on that.

Sanity is by no means just conventional reality, which stuffs its ears against the new and prevents fresh validations.

QUESTION: Do you ever have patients who don't want to use the Gestalt techniques?

DR. SCHOEN: Yes. And I don't insist on them. The techniques take a certain boldness in self-dramatization. Have you noticed how many Gestalt therapists like to be theatrical, present company included?

One patient, for instance, flatly refused to put her father—a troubling authoritarian to her—in the "empty chair." All right! But a time came when she was having a very upsetting moment with me. She's an accomplished violinist, and she was willing, at my invitation, to play a violin-piano sonata with me. Then, near the beginning, she froze! She said, "It's amazing, but I feel you're like my father, different as you are, and I can't play a note." We left the instruments, and I encouraged her to tell me just how she *did not want* me to be like her father—for instance, "I don't want you to be disrespectful of me," and so on. And now she was willing to "do Gestalt," and she felt the better for it. Here, you see, the technique fit unobtrusively, without any falsifications of the real scene.

QUESTION: It is interesting that you played music with her. Do you use music often?

DR. SCHOEN: Sometimes I play for a person if he or she resembles a certain piece of music to me: Schumann's portraits in *Carnaval* lend themselves to that. But I use the music because it happens to be a particular expression of mine. What counts is whatever expresses you, as the therapist. *Your* responses—not piano, art, theater, or any other mode of expression—are the real instrument of the therapy. That's why our training centers at first on your own freedom to respond.

QUESTION: What are most people coming to you about these days? Is there anything characteristic about them? We seem to be in a strange period. There aren't campus riots now. There seems to be a giant lull. Particularly, what are young people who come to you like? Is there a theme?

OTHER QUESTION (*with laughter*): Yes, A-B-C problems. What are the big five?

DR. SCHOEN: It's an interesting question. Well, many people come for the reasons that they have "always" come, through my experience of eighteen years. They are deeply discontent, or they are plain freaked out. For instance, a fellow appeared three months ago saying: "I don't understand! I told everyone I was going to London on my vacation. I looked forward to it, went to the San Francisco Airport, and I did not get on the plane! I don't know why I didn't get on the plane. And I got so freaked out that I called you up." All right, I don't know that this is among the top five! Certainly, it could have happened eighteen years ago too.

But I believe I can say something about a "characteristic" problem of today's youth, compared with, say, the patients of twenty-five years ago, among them myself. Back then, there was a frequent fearfulness of impulse life, combined with a hold on external structures—socioeconomic, career, marriage. Children of repressions, we *held ourselves in*. Today, many young people I see, while comparably as confused in their living as we were then, find it simple to *go with impulses*. As children of a permissive style of child-rearing, they easily "move into different spaces," as they say. Today, without social protest and riots, there's even less focus for their energy. Literally, the youth drift a lot, without ties to school, job, place, or person. They are overly inclined to let go of themselves, while we were overly inclined to hold on. It's as though all the jigsaw-puzzle-piece parts of their lives are spread out wide and they don't know how to "get it all together"—a phrase in common use today. But with us, pieces were closer in and often buried under one another; and the job was to uncover them, look at them, and then place them in the picture.

QUESTION: Will you discuss responsibility more? I'm confused. I've always assumed that responsibility is accepting that you've created the thing: that if someone punches me in the face, I've caused him to punch me. Isn't that right?

DR. SCHOEN: No! Responsibility, in Gestalt, *doesn't* mean "being responsible for someone else's behavior." You're responsible for "being punched in the face," being there to receive the punch. That's your behavior. Do you see the difference? And it is only to your own responses that your responsibility applies.

A patient of mine who was annoyed at his girlfriend for getting hysterically upset at him said to me, "Stephen, I don't need that!" And I answered, "Matthew, you *do* need that!" Do you see how quick he was to turn away from his own response? It takes two to dance the dance of any interaction—you are setting up something when your partner is "hysterically upset," and her hysteria then alerts your own next response. On both fronts, as provoker of her hysteria and as responder to it, this man's chief response was to deny.

In fact, I'm impressed by how much we have to learn from others' responses to us, particularly if the responses are hard to deal with, and how we are especially aware of those responses which are both difficult *and* within range of our mastery. It's as though we are always readying ourselves for what comes along. In fact, the man I've mentioned was readying himself to confront his own habit of denial; and he *was* interested in an alternative.

QUESTION: Doesn't it all come down to realizing that we always have a choice in response? And this leads us to take responsibility for our choice.

DR. SCHOEN: I see what you mean. Subjectively, I believe it's natural to say we have a choice, up to the point that we make it! Then it becomes inevitable, unalterable! At the least, we often have the *feeling* that we make choices. And yet when we live well, we sense that we are fulfilling our nature; and this has the flavor of the thing which feels *so* right we could not choose to do anything else! As Dante says of men who are alive in God: "In his will is our peace." Anything else is impossible for them, as a plant grows without choice towards the sun.

My own way of working involves, as you've seen tonight, a lot of imagery. Metaphors and analogies come to me easily. I find them clarifying and stimulating, and I use them often with my patients.

I want to make a final pitch for the excitement of Gestalt work! The flair of Gestalt is, without denying any data, still to be affirmative: anxiety, for instance, is a sign of *life*, if one distressfully felt! And the Gestalt affirmation is always of life *free of external control.* Ecologically, we know that even environmental controls designed to be benevolent can end up as a loss to nature; for instance, straightening waterways in Germany, to improve the transportation of goods and to enhance irrigation, finally lowered the water table and decreased the fertility of the soil. Over against this, remember, the principle in Gestalt is: control nothing. And in our era—when, with dubious motives of benevolence, more and more effective controls of behavior, through drugs, psychological manipulation, and political measures are likely to be the prevailing cultural standard for a long time—Gestalt is contributing a different testament, which opposes that standard for the sake of individual freedom.

Women and Gestalt Awareness

Lois Brien, Ph.D., and
Cynthia Sheldon, M.S.W.

In a short number of years, Gestalt therapy has come to be used in a variety of settings by large numbers of therapists in all parts of this country and Europe as well. At the Gestalt Institute of San Francisco, new applications of Gestalt were constantly being made. The beginnings of our Gestalt Institute work with women lay, like most beginnings, in our unconscious or out-of-awareness zones. At this time there were seven of us women active in the Institute: Paula Bottome, Lois Brien, Elaine Kepner, Stella Resnick, Janie Rhyne, Cynthia Sheldon, and Celia Thompson-Taupin. Most of us had spent a great deal of time coleading Gestalt groups with the men of the Institute, but not with each other. We realized that we didn't know one another—and wanted to.

Thus the first women's workshop was scheduled in 1968—led by all of us. The desire to work together and know one another, and understand our similarities and common experiences, opened a new door of awareness. Until this time we had all done a lot of personal introspection and work on ourselves, learning about the roles we played and how we stopped ourselves from living more fully. However, the impact of the sociological aspects of women's roles in our culture, made so obvious now by the women's movement, had not emerged as a large social force in the world or as an awareness in us.

Here in the Bay area in 1968 were the elements of great changes. Berkeley's radical days of large demonstrations had changed the University of California in some ways and had begun to subside. Esalen Institute and other workshop centers were popular and flooding the area with new ways of being. Fritz Perls was preparing his Gestalt approach to social change and moving to Canada. The Gestalt Institute of San Francisco was training professional therapists; Third World leaders who were emerging in self-help clinics, rap groups, and the like; and professionals in other fields, such as teaching, art, nursing, law, and even the sciences.

As our female consciousness emerged, we began to view the California setting differently. Many women, including ourselves, had become dissatisfied with our noncombatant, sideline roles in the radical-political scene. We were the housekeepers; men were on the front lines leading the marches and rallies, while women were in the back office making coffee and licking stamps. It was the same in the growth movement. Men, well-known and not so well-known, were billed as leaders of all kinds of workshops—workshops that promised new aliveness, freedom, awareness, physical release, satori, and so on. Women *were* getting in touch with their static, subordinate roles, freeing their energies as promised yet still falling prey to the charisma of the male leaders. For a woman, the next best thing to becoming a lover of an Esalen leader was becoming a secretary at Esalen. If you were lucky, maybe you would get to do massage or dance "therapy," appropriate women's work.

Such was the 1968 setting as we viewed it. Over half of us women at the Institute changed our marital status, while many of the women we were treating also were in the throes of divorce and separation. Both personally and in our work we were facing such issues as how to feel okay being divorced, how to survive as a single parent, and how to change the social/female stigmas that women are less competent therapists, less intelligent, and lacking emotional balance. The loss and pain experienced by some of the women, many of whom were dependent on their male relationships for emotional and financial support, was profound. We, our clients and ourselves, worked together on new ways to carve out life-styles in which we could feel responsible, independent, and good about ourselves.

The men, too, were changing. In California, as in other parts of the country, many men were rebelling against the establishment, either refusing to win the family financial bread by taking an unsatisfying job or dropping out of existing jobs. Men in their thirties and forties were leaving well-paying jobs as engineers, accountants, business executives, and teachers in order to "find themselves," to develop their creativity in ways that fitted each one personally instead of automatically fulfilling the customary male role of breadwinner and family supporter. The result of their dropping out was usually a substantial loss in pay—which, of course, affected the future security of their wives and children. The old models of woman-man relationships were changing, upsetting the balance and frequently influencing couples to divorce and separate.

Thus women found themselves faced with changing family structures that included less financial security and loss of their men. In addition, they were facing the disillusionment with the radical political movement and the growth scene, where they were second-class citizens seeking the love and approval of the male *honchos* and gurus. Finally, some women began to see how they bought into the top-dog male attitude and ignored each other almost completely. Women discovered that they were second-class citizens to each other, avoiding really knowing and appreciating one another. Now women are discovering many ways in which they can help each other, everything from being nurturing and supportive to being intellectually and emotionally stimulating. The cultural myth that only a "good man" can be there for a woman emotionally, intellectually, and financially no longer holds. We now know that women can be there for women too.

This is the complex milieu that fostered the beginnings of our Gestalt work with women—unconscious and searching at first, slowly coming more into focused awareness. Our goals emerged from our experience. From leading Gestalt workshops for women we expanded to include ongoing women's groups, a low-fee drop-in group, and far more women (including women couples) in our private practices.

At this point we will describe the process of Gestalt awareness and then relate it to our work with women specifically. The therapeutic process of Gestalt awareness focuses on *how* we behave, think, feel, and how we enhance or stop our aliveness and life energy. We effectively use only a small percentage of our potential; the rest we block with illness, muscle tightness, and the social games we play. We adopt inflexible "shoulds" and "should nots" that may not fit us.

An adolescent girl is told that she shouldn't have sexual relations until she is either married or twenty-one. This rule may or may not fit her internal makeup. If she complies despite her true sexual wants, she must consciously tighten her abdominal and vaginal muscles, stopping the flow of energy to the pelvis, legs, and feet.

Becoming habitual and forgotten in later years, this can cause abdominal distress, sexual fridigity, and pelvic tightness. She may even come to be labeled "hysterical" instead of simply viewed as someone whose energy is literally blocked from going to her feet!

Another example is the "good girl." She has been taught that nice girls are seen and not heard. This rule leads to blocking in many areas—throat, jaw, chest—tightening her muscles to stop words from coming out of her mouth. Many other feelings—despair, joy, sadness, anger—may be locked in her body as well. The "good girl's" ability to experience life (to take in feelings and sensations and to savor them slowly) is probably poor and limited by the rigid muscular armor that prevents all but "nice" feelings from showing. She may be perceived by others as shallow and phony.

So restricting emotions and blocking muscular discharge inhibit the use of potential. Gestalt awareness training encourages women to experiment, to challenge their social introjects (their "should" systems), and to pick the rules and values they *want* to live by, creating their own structures and finding their own style of aliveness.

The Gestalt work that we have done with women and their problems is best presented in a series of vignettes from the experiences themselves.

In 1969, Lois led a women's group at Bridge Mountain Foundation in the Santa Cruz Mountains of northern California. "I sat there and looked around that group of nineteen women—I was looking at nineteen different styles and ways to be a woman. Up to that point I thought women were supposed to be pretty much the way television and newspaper advertisements pictured us. You were either blonde, blue-eyed, slim, and sexy, or you were not a woman. I was simply overwhelmed with the differences! It had never occurred to me that there were so many ways that women appeared—and in spite of the wide range of differences, they were *all* women."

Cynthia Sheldon, who was a participant in a women's weekend in 1967, had a similar experience. "After being together for two days, most of the women felt relaxed and good about themselves. Boxes of costumes and materials were present, and each was encouraged to find that which fit her in particular. As the time passed, each began to dance. Nobody was trying to be who they were not. Their ways of moving were different, as were their ways of looking and their gestures. Their outfits expressed so many aspects: sultry, sweet, languid, soft, tough, cute, brash, solid, matronly, giddy, seductive. All the old stereotypes of how a woman should be made no sense to me anymore. Each one was incredibly beautiful."

A Gestalt workshop held in 1969 was called "The Man-and-Woman Thing." The women met separately for part of the weekend, and during that time one young woman expressed some deep sadness that touched the entire group. Another woman went to her and held her. This touched the group again. Others cried, and still others came and held them. The experience profoundly moved them all. Afterwards, they discussed how hard it was to allow themselves to be taken care of by a woman, how scared they were to feel like a little girl with a woman, how frightened they were about their sensual feelings for women. And they talked about how often they would turn to men rather than women for this kind of nurturing.

Another women's group met weekly for ten sessions with a daylong videotaped session at the end. Most of these women were in college and graduate school and in their mid-twenties. During the time together, most expressed their dislike for themselves. They didn't fit the cultural stereotype of the desirable woman. Each felt that something was wrong with her body: one's hips were too large, another's hair was too curly, someone's belly protruded, and so on. At the final videotape session everyone donned costumes, laughed and danced and played—and many took off all their clothes. In watching themselves on the videotape monitor and seeing themselves move and dance with and without costumes, most of them realized how attractive they were—not just physically, but in the ways they moved and laughed and played. There was a strong sense of sisterhood and sharing as each one began a process of unhooking herself from the cultural female stereotypical "shoulds."

Again in the late 1960s, another women's weekend with Gestalt leaders was held in the country. Janie Rhyne, a Gestalt art therapist, had each woman make an image in clay of herself at that moment. Using Gestalt, one woman was asked to role-play her image, which reminded her of her vagina. She was nervous about sharing this personal experience and overwhelmed with the new sensations and feelings that she had discovered. She had never before focused this kind of attention on any of her body parts. It is hard to say what she specifically received from this experience other than that it opened a new way for her to understand herself. She became more in touch with her entire being as she learned to focus her awareness elsewhere than in her head.

These five groups we've described used the permissive experiencing modality of Gestalt to encourage women to risk new ways. Many cultural "shoulds" were shed like the old skin of a snake.

The women's movement has helped highlight the glaring "shoulds" that so many of us have taken for granted:

A woman's place should be in the home.
A woman should marry.
A woman should bear and raise children.
A woman should be her husband's emotional support.
A woman shouldn't disagree with her husband: he and the children come first.
A desirable woman worth catching (by a man) should have a glamorous body—i.e., as modeled after *Vogue* magazine and other fashion setters.
A woman shouldn't be aggressive.

In Gestalt women's groups we are not out to show women that the above dicta are invalid. We attempt to get women to look closely at each dictum she has adopted, to see if it nourishes her or whether she swallowed it without tasting it. The important point is that she can *choose*; usually women don't know that.

One of the problems we've encountered with women who are in the women's movement is that they've adopted a new set of "shoulds," swallowed them just like the old ones, without choosing them specifically to fit themselves. Some of these new dicta are:

A woman should be independent.
A woman should work.
A woman shouldn't spend time on her appearance.
A woman should be aggressive and stand up for herself first.
A woman should be bisexual.
A woman should never play any old female games.
A woman should never spend time with a male chauvinist.

These rules can be as undigested as the others. The point is for women to take responsibility for themselves and for their own rules, making sure that they fit and are digestible. What *I* can digest may make *you* nauseous.

The following edited transcript from a session with a woman who came for some Gestalt work will illustrate our point about finding the way that fits:

(Diane, a young married accountant in a small public agency, came into therapy distraught about what to do with her marriage.)

DIANE: If I stay with my husband, I'll get more and more dull and uninteresting. I'll become middle-class and ordinary. We don't see other people very much, and I'm afraid of falling into the ordinary female housewife role.

THERAPIST: What do you think you want?

DIANE: In order not to be dull, I suppose I shouldn't live with one person. I should share myself with a lot of people. I shouldn't be jealous of my husband's working all the time. But I am. My friends think I should leave him, since he doesn't pay much attention to me. They think I should move into their commune, where they are trying to be free.

THERAPIST: Are you aware of how often you've used the word "should"? "Shoulds" usually are demands that we pick up from our environment, and seldom do they come from within us. One way to test out what is yours and what isn't is to substitute "I want" for those "shoulds." Try it.

DIANE: (*She tries many*) I want to share myself with many other people. I don't want to live with just one person. I want to leave my husband because he isn't paying enough attention to me. I want to live in a commune to become free. I don't want to be jealous. I do want to be jealous. I don't want to be middle-class. I want to be ordinary, and middle-class.

THERAPIST: What happened when you tried these on? Did your body give you any messages?

DIANE: Yes, sometimes my stomach would grip tightly. I can see that some fit and others don't.

(After much trial and error, Diane checked each message to see which ones felt right for her. This is the list she came up with.)

I don't want to share myself with a lot of other people.
I want to live with one person.
I want to be interesting, and sometimes it's okay to be ordinary.
I'm not sure at this time what I want with my husband.

Diane found that when she turned into her own internal process and took responsibility for what she wanted, she moved from the "should" levels down to her feelings about herself and her husband. She felt relieved and ready to take a closer look at her real situation. Often the "shoulds" blur the actuality of life.

Another result of working with women in the groups we've described is that, through using the experiential modality of Gestalt, many women come in touch with very different and exciting facets of themselves. Unfortunately, so many people who adopt roles to play are often like dolls or cartoon characters; they react the same no matter what the conditions are. The following is an example of such a situation:

(Holly is a thirty-year-old "girl" who is about to break up with her boyfriend. She speaks in a high-pitched, childlike, breathy voice.)

HOLLY: I don't know what to do about his leaving. I guess I feel hurt. I don't know what to do.

THERAPIST: Say that to him. Imagine he's facing you now.

HOLLY (*her voice is high, with no feeling coming through*): I feel hurt. Where will I go now?

THERAPIST: Holly, what do you hear in your voice?

HOLLY: Well, it sounds sort of high and whiny. Is that what you mean?

THERAPIST: I'm aware there's not much strength in the sound of your voice. Try dropping your voice down around the level of your navel and talk to him from there.

HOLLY (*in a high voice again*): I can't do it.

THERAPIST: Tell him that, then.

HOLLY (*voice is a bit stronger, and she laughs*): I can't talk to you in a low voice, Sam.

THERAPIST: Let's do this standing up. Put your hands on your belly, and see if you can hear your voice coming from there.

HOLLY: Sam, I feel hurt.

THERAPIST: A little louder.

HOLLY: Now I feel angry. Sam, I'm angry. I'm angry at you.

THERAPIST: Put your voice down a little bit lower. You're really getting it now.

HOLLY (*her voice is low now and strong; there is no question about how she is feeling*): I feel pissed off at you, Sam. Goddamn you, you motherfucker. You walked out on me without saying a damn thing. You treated me like scum. I hate you. Get out of my life, and leave me alone. You make me sick. You're chicken shit. You don't even have the guts to face me. You make me sick.

While these feelings were scary, Holly was very exhilarated by the experience. She discovered a core of assertiveness and strength that she had been completely unaware of. Experiencing this kind of power meant she had to change her breathy, girlish image of herself.

Not everyone opens up into a new area of themselves quite this fast. But it does happen again and again. Fritz Perls refers to this process as getting in touch with the "holes in our personality." We refer to this process as learning to increase the repertoire of feelings, experiences, and roles that we have available to meet the world with. So many women are limited. They don't have many feelings available or many ways to assert themselves positively. Our cultural roles have been quite restricting. (Just look at how women's clothing restricts their movements. Skirts are tight and short, and shoes are high and immobilizing except if you walk in a very patterned way!) It is our contention that women must add to their behaviors and styles or they will suffocate and starve. It's no accident that so many women have run to therapists for help. (Unfortunately, traditional male-dominated psychiatry has often only reinforced the suffocating roles women have been locked into.) We are trying to expand women's repertoires, not help them adjust and shrink into the existing molds. Gestalt therapy is inherently expansionistic—constantly encouraging women to stretch their minds and make use of all relevant input, so that they may come to their own experience.

And another phenomenon is occurring with women everywhere who are getting together in groups and who are working in Gestalt ways: as women are getting to know each other in new ways and as they are becoming more alive, they are also becoming more exciting and interesting to one another. Women find this surprising. "I never thought a woman could teach me anything." "Anytime I was at a party, I'd talk with the men as they had more to say." This is changing. Women are entering such male-dominated professions as the law, management, banking, and even the building trades. They are returning to school to study all manner of things. They now have more to offer each other than an exchange of recipes or childrearing practices. Women are seeking each other out for intellectual stimulation and emotional support, and for fun and companionship as well. Instead of restricting themselves to fifty percent of the world—men—for contact, they now have the whole world. And that is a very exciting cultural opening!

Gestalt awareness is an incredibly powerful tool for turning women on to themselves, and away from the stereotyped paper dolls many used to be. As women come to enjoy their intelligence, accept their physical bodies, and use their emotionality in creative ways, they become, in essence, exciting new beings.

A Gestalt Way of Using Language

Paula Bottome, Ph.D.

Gestalt language is the language of here and now, of immediacy and life. Words and content are shaping my perceptions and awareness, which are process. Words and usages, like so many of the apparent givens of my life, are alterable. Language shapes my awareness and, at the same time, I shape a language. How I use language determines what I am experiencing.

I create language by picking up a slang word ("stylin' "), a phrase ("gettin' it together"), dropping a word ("shall"), and taking a Yiddish word or two (*kvetch, knosh*). I listen to the young, the drugged, the academic, and the marginal. I take from them the words and phrases that I want for my own. This is one of the ways I create an ever more subtle and expressive language for myself. I attend to words and usage, molding and modifying them toward the forms of life and experience I want to have and to share. In this process I am joined by the other speakers of American English, and together we bring forth a language. By consciously participating in this linguistic process, I become a creator of the evolving language and thus of the thought and world view that human beings design together.

In order to change conventional usage to promote immediacy, I am learning the linguistic structures that allow and encourage this experience. I listen to myself and change my speech to allow the fullest expression of me and who I am. I have found that a sensitivity to pronoun usage is an important part of this process. According to Webster's Unabridged Dictionary, pronouns have little or no fixed meaning except one of "relation and limitation." This emptiness of meaning makes the way I use pronouns a sensitive indicator of my psychological states.

Current American usage allows several devices for avoiding the immediacy of "I" and the self-responsibility that "I" creates. I can avoid "I" by saying "you."

> You know, when you walk down the street and the rain beats on your umbrella and the wind blows you around.

I was taught that I am rude when I express my experience as happening to an "I" or a "me."

> I know when I walk down the street and the rain beats on my umbrella and the wind blows me around.

I know when I say "I" that I am awake. I feel solid and substantial, willing to stand up and be counted as one of the creators and participants rather than an observer for whom events happen to "you" and "it" and "people" and "one." Saying "I," I create myself as a subject rather than as an object, an actor rather than a victim.

I can avoid "I" by saying "it."

> It hurts.
> It's cold.
> It's not funny.

In interpersonal dialogue "it" is a doubly confusing pronoun, for "it" often refers to the other person and is substituted for "you" as well as for "I."

I don't like it.

The use of "it" for "I" and "you" in conversation results in such a welter of "its" without antecedents that dialogue is reduced to gibberish. Fritz Perls said, "Change the 'it' to 'I' or 'you.' Personalize in order to bring the present into your words."

"You," referring to the immediate other person, is as often avoided as "I." A much-used replacement for "you" is "that," as in "that's right." Saying "you're right" is lively and engaging. Saying "that's right" is withholding and withdrawing. This use of "that" is an example of a linguistic structure promoting depersonalization so subtly and naturally that most people fail to notice it. This usage builds between people an unconscious and invisible barrier that many feel and label alienation. The spark, the contact, of I-you is gone, replaced by it-that, anonymous conversations between unidentified objects.

It hurts.
That's all right.
Where is everybody?

Contemporary English makes no distinction between "you," the intimate other person, and "you," the impersonal others addressed by television announcers. The absence of a familiar form of the pronoun "you"—namely, "thou"—makes it impossible to convey the ideas of Martin Buber in contemporary American English. His translators retrieved the archaic form and called his book *I and Thou*. This is an example of how feelings shape the language we speak and how the language in time comes to shape certain of our experiences. As an American, I could easily have grown up unaware that there was once a word ("thou") for saying "you" to intimates and children.

"That" and "there" are pronouns whose usage is a distancing maneuver. Like "it," "that" is an overused word, for not only is "that" used to replace "you," "that" is often used instead of "this." "This" is the demonstrative pronoun of the present. "There" is the word for away, distant.

I want this (here).
I want that (there).

I hear many people wonder out loud whether they will ever "get there," when what they mean is "get here." "Here" is where the action is. As Gertrude Stein said, "There is no there there." Only when "there" becomes a "here" do I leave fantasy land. What is the point of discussing "that" and "there" when I am animate and vivid saying "this" and "here"? Listening, I often hear people spontaneously change from "that there" to "this here" as they become more animated and involved in their stories.

Verbs express action and states of being. The present tense of verbs is the tense of life. Past and future are fantasy, for I live now. Past and future tenses allow me to imagine I am detached from my statements. This detachment allows me to perceive myself as a victim and therefore to avoid taking responsibility for me. How can I be responsible for what my mother did when I was (am) six months old? I am, though, for by talking about my mother, I am creating her now. The appearance of separation in time allowed by the past and future tenses promotes the myth of objectivity in conversation. I am saying "I am" regardless of whether I am talking about ancient Rome or a sore finger. When the present tense is abandoned for linguistic conventions, I continue to hear people saying, "This concerns me now. I am in this fantasy now." Like the pounding of the surf, "now" sounds behind all words —with the evocative magic of giving the past and future a solidity that is ephemeral.

I create a fantasy of the future now.
You create a memory of the past now.
Now we create a group fantasy and call it nostalgia.

American English contains adverbs that pretend to qualify when they disparage. "I'm just a housewife" is a classic usage of this kind. Contrast "I am a housewife" with "I'm just a housewife." Used this way, "just" is a put-down that takes away the power of the statement. "Only" is used in a similar and derogatory way.

He's only visiting.
I'm only joking.

"Always" and "never" often mask accusations.

You never come.
You always say that.

By using these eternity words, I change a descriptive statement ("You're leaving the dirty dishes") into a guilt-smearing remark ("You always leave the dirty dishes").

You never kiss me.
We never talk.

Using these words is a dramatic device, like rolling up the big guns.

"But" is a word I am dropping from my language. "But" takes away, separates, and disintegrates in a sneaky way. "Yes, but" is a classic game discussed by Eric Berne, and anyone who has played "yes, but" with awareness knows what a debilitating dialogue this game creates. "I love you, but" is another mixed message that leads to confusion and chaos in interpersonal relations.

The use of "but" allows me to give with one hand and take away with the other. "But" makes equivocation respectable. By replacing "but" with "and," I maintain the possibilities in my situation and begin to integrate.

"And" is an inclusive word, a statement of relationship that serves to link, to level, and to connect. "And" is nonjudgmental and allows human beings the variety and choice inherent in life.

As the Gestalt approach is discovered by a large group of people, I see a tendency to turn the attitudes and insights of Gestalt into rules and ultimately values. A clear example of this appears in the language with the popularity of the phrases "I feel that" and "I feel like." Expressions of feeling (emotion) are valued in Gestalt work and the growth movement generally. "I feel that" is a way of using the word "feel" without expressing an emotion.

I feel that you are sad now.
I feel that you want to hurt me.
I feel that they are happy together.

The speaker in these sentences is sharing fantasies rather than emotions.

I imagine you are sad now.
I think you want to hurt me.
I pretend they are happy together.

Many people shy away from feeling statements, which are usually short and succinct.

I feel good.
I feel soft.
I am happy.

"I feel like" at least retains and makes explicit the metaphorical nature of language and often gives the listener insight into a speaker's feelings—for example, "I feel like I did when I was six." This statement is not an expression of emotion regardless of how evocative it may be of feelings. The dialogue resulting from this statement might go like this:

I feel like I did when I was six.
How do you feel now?
I feel small and helpless.

The last is a statement of emotion.

Another process occurring with the expansion of Gestalt is the emergence of new "should's." The words "should," "must," and "have to" stand for introjected values. Introjected values are information concerning good and bad that I have taken in and refused to assimilate and make part of me; they are unexamined and unobserved "do's" and "don't's" that I carry around like lumps of undigested food in my gut. So pervasive is introjection that many ideas that in their content suggest organismic self-regulation are internalized as "shoulds," new rules and part of a new morality.

I should say "I."
I should let my organism regulate itself.
I should be aware of my language.

The "shoulding" process is my attempt to overwhelm my self-regulating organism and to shape me in a pattern decided upon by someone else. The harm done to human beings by forcing them to live by rules other than their own feelings is inestimable.

Rather than "shoulding" each other, we would be more honest if we spoke the language of desire. Contrast "I want you to clean up your room" with "You should clean up your room." The present acceptance of "should" allows parents to pit the word of God against the desire of the child.

Parent: You should . . .
Child: I want . . .

This usage loads power onto the powerful.

Using "should" and supporting introjected values, I disrupt my ability to contact and respond in a delicate and flowing way. When I am here balancing on the now, I am occupied and involved, and "should's" are superfluous.

Where Do Your Lines Lead? Gestalt Art Groups

Celia Thompson-Taupin, M.A.T.

In my work leading Gestalt art groups, I have been struck by the rapid engagement in nonverbal exercises of people with highly developed verbal capacity. Even the simplest, most abstract game often produces fresh awareness. In fact, messages from within may emerge more clearly when the verbal, thinking part of us has little opportunity to figure out and plan.

What is going on when a person discovers how he is feeling as he draws, moves, pantomimes, makes noises? How is he discovering himself? Why can't some people play games? What are games? These are the kinds of questions I reflect on after art groups. Many current psychologies provide human models and vocabularies to describe the internal dynamics of such "intra-action," and I assume that all of them are open to amendment and synthesis as the body of knowledge about human experience expands. After describing group sessions that prompt such questions, I will offer brief theoretical considerations about what may be happening.

I would like to express my appreciation to my co-leaders in some of the group sessions described—Janie Rhyne, Abe Levitsky, and Robert Liikala.

Of many possible games, the line game is one of the simplest; yet during the past year, several groups have found it unexpectedly rich. The group participants were all active, productive, basically healthy persons interested in expanding their awareness of themselves and others through creative experience. The line game serves as a vehicle for sharing experiences and ideas that are not dependent on the particular technique. Its modest rules of play may reemphasize its essential unimportance.*

The line game is played by tacking a large sheet of paper on the wall and having on hand a basket of crayons or pieces of chalk of various colors. One person at a time is "it." That person comes up to the paper and is told, "Select a color and draw a line or a shape." That being done, he is told, "Now another, with a different color." I usually ask the person to make the sound and movement of each line or shape. Other group members are encouraged to mimic and get into the spirit of how each line feels to the person who is "it." At this point, many choices are open. One possibility is the "gestalting" of the two lines or shapes by "it." Another, used in the episodes below, is to say to "it," "Now use people in the group to be your lines and dramatize what is going on. You are the director of the play for the next few minutes—and you can also be one of the characters. It's your show." What happens from this moment on is rarely dull and often involving for the whole group.

Rocking Valley

When Jim came forward, he drew a strong brown sine wave and a bit of blue above. He selected eight

* For a discussion of the pitfalls of depending on technique, see Joel Latner, *The Gestalt Therapy Book* (New York: The Julian Press, 1973), pp. 187–193.

people and asked them to form a valley by facing in pairs and linking hands. They began to sway and hum. He called for wind. Three people blew, gracefully waving their arms over the valley. I asked him if he would like to lie down in his valley, which he did with obvious delight, being rocked with his eyes closed, listening to the wind makers chant. The game came to a natural, quiet close.

Rather than pursuing his need for nurturance or support, I let it be. My way of playing the game is to shift into therapy modes only if "it" leads in that direction or if there is evident discomfort that invites further interaction. This seems to engender a group atmosphere that can be more relaxed and spontaneous, freeing people from second-guessing how their actions might be interpreted in some psychological framework.

Get Off My Back!

Kathy drew an orange corkscrew and above it an arc of purple. As she directed the group to embody her pattern, we found the corkscrew was carefree and skipping, but the purple was a heavy, constricting inhibitor. She asked several people to push down on her back as she struggled to move freely. "It's my father," she gasped, "pushing, holding, being serious and sad. I had no idea when I drew the lines." The group dispersed to the sidelines, and Kathy chose to work in a Gestalt manner on her internalized father, who interfered with many aspects of her current life.

Phsst . . . Aahhh

Nancy first drew a green spiral, then a wiggly orange line at an angle to the spiral. She spiritedly demonstrated that the spiral moved as a fluid wave, with a leisurely "aahhh," and the wiggly line was a jerky, hopping dance with abrupt turns, accompanied by staccato "zzzt phsst" noises. Soon the room was bursting with gentle somersaulters and frantic hoppers. At the peak of the action, Nancy called a halt, saying "Now switch. That's it—now I can feel it . . . " After the game subsided, she reported a feeling of calm, steady energy inside. She added that she often wore herself out by getting tense and jumping from one thing to another; yet, deeper within, she experienced much greater steadiness. By seeing and physically experiencing the contrast between these two states, she felt clearer about how to use her energy with greater flow and purpose.

Pillars and Volcanoes

After a long, intense pause, Pat got up and drew a thick vertical blue line, saying, "Same old me." On the right hand side, two concentric red circles made a doughnut shape. To the three people she selected for the blue, she explained, "You are pure, cool, remote, and meditative." To the three reds she said, "You are volcanoes, erupting and running over with lava and being totally unruly and passionate." After surveying the resulting scene, she decided, "I'll be one of the volcanoes—that's where it's at, anyway." The pure pillars began to hum in harmony with each other, moving their arms above their heads or clasping hands prayerfully. The volcanoes lept and hissed, waving their arms and sticking their tongues out with loud noises. Pat started pushing the pillars; the other volcanoes followed her lead. The pillars' job, a difficult one, was to ignore this meddling and stay in a contemplative mood. Pat said, "Speak!" The blues intoned, "Calmness . . . tranquility, air . . . sunlight . . ." while the reds called out words of violence and anger. When Pat ordered,

"Sex!" the volcanoes approached the pillars, making lascivious movements and come-ons. One of the blues became a red and wrestled with her attacker on the floor.

For a moment I stepped out of my role as a blue to experience the scene as a whole. The intensity was remarkable. Finally the energy died down, and the blues regrouped to complain about the interference of the unruly reds. After the group panted to seated quiescense, I asked Pat, "What's happening now?"

"I really see myself more clearly than ever in this. I just can't get into the spiritual part of me and feel right in it. I understand the other, passionate self, but not the spiritual."

"How do you experience the spiritual part?"

"Ram Dass really turns me on. When I listen to him or read him, I want to give up everything and follow him. But the other side of myself says that's ridiculous —I'm not that. I can imagine myself going into a nunnery, cutting myself off completely from the rest of my life."

Pat put her spiritual self on the pillow and started sentences with the phrase "If I honored you" ("If I honored you, I would stop everything I am doing. I don't know what would happen after that"). To her ordinary self, the spiritual side said, "If I honored you . . . " and stopped. "I cannot, do not, honor that self."

Suspecting the dichotomy had more to do with St. Paul and the Calvinists than with Ram Dass and the Indian gurus, I proposed that she take a third position, the complete human experience. "What do you feel from there?" She sat silent on the third pillow for quite a while and said, "I feel like a wise old man." I asked, "Not a wise old woman?"

"No, definitely a wise old man. Wow! That's where

it's *really* at—I have always given all the wisdom to men."

"Have you ever known a wise old woman?"

"No, and I've wanted to."

One of the group members suggested, "Speak to each of us, and say 'If you were a wise old woman . . .' and tell each of us what we would be like."

Pat made the rounds:

To C.: "If you were a wise old woman, you would stand at the crossroads and, as people came by, you'd help them across without making any claim on them."

To L.: " . . . you would be a Mother Earth, with fruits and children flowing from you."

To J.: " . . . you would be a sphinx. You would know the answers to the riddles but tell them in such a way that people would have to discover the meanings for themselves."

To B.: " . . . you would be the headmistress of an information exchange, making sure that everybody had all the facts they needed."

To N.: " . . . you would simply endure with the ageless quality of ongoing life."

To J. A.: "If you were a wise old man, I could bury my head in your lap."

I handed her a mirror. She looked in it and said, "I'm a bitch," paused, and tried again. "If I were a wise old woman—block, block! I can't do it." Then she looked long and earnestly, closed her eyes, and said, "If I were a wise old woman, I'd just *be*." She moved back against the wall and was quiet for a long time. Then she expressed a feeling of longing and sadness.

I suggested that we gather in the center of the room and create the collective Wise Old Woman of our group. The eight of us sat in a close circle holding hands in silence. Something very strong started happening; several found tears running down their cheeks, others trembled. Very gradually we disengaged hands, and after a long pause each woman described her own experience of those minutes.

Pat said she had never felt so much support before from other women, but added, "I am only crawling, *crawling*, toward my spiritual self."

One woman said she didn't feel anything in the circle, although she wanted to, and what should she do? We sang for her (and for Pat) a chorus of the Beatles' song "Let It Be."

Pat mused at the end of the session, "I never realized how much power I had given men. All during college I always chose men profs, read things men wrote, wanted to be like a man. When we planned this group, I was disappointed when it turned out to be all women. I thought it would be horribly dull because nothing ever happens without men."

Pat's dichotomy between spiritual-female-passive-nonsexual and worldly-male-active-passionate touched each of us, although we may not have built up the same groupings of stereotypes. Her very apt personal fantasy for each woman seemed to cut through the rigid categories in which she cornered herself and perhaps helped her to experience the support of sisterhood. She has begun a long process of work.

Rite of Passage

In a weekend workshop, Bev had worked with the group on her feelings of being overshadowed and undervalued as the wife of a distinguished scholar whose intellectual world seemed to have little appreciation for her intuitive, expressive style, puckishness, and spiritual searching. Prior to her turn, the group had shared several lively line games. The atmosphere was open for action.

Bev selected a piece of chalk, backed off across the room, and charged the paper on the wall, making a *wham* dot. "Me!" she yelled, circling it vigorously. She danced around to people in the group, laughing and pointing to her chest. "I'm *me*! I'm *me*!" She got everyone up and moving, directing them in an infectious dance, repeating with relish, "It's *my* show! It's *my show*!"* People moved with one another fluidly and in rhythm, with an apparently very high level of contact. When Bev's strength waned and the dance ended, we started chanting slowly around the room in a sequential pattern that overlapped like a round, "Iii 'mmmmmm mmmeeeeeee. . . . " Bev came to rest in the middle, glowing. The chant, having personal meaning for each chanter, undulated around her—a validation of her personhood. I surprised myself by getting up, walking to her slowly, raising her shirt, and making a solemn circle around her belly button with a red pen.

"This calls for a ritual," someone said. Bev lay trusting and spread-eagle on a mat. We gathered around, still chanting "I'm me" in a continuous slow flow. The atmosphere was one of respect, even reverence. The pen was passed from one person to another, and each added a stroke to Bev's belly design, which became a mandala radiating out from her belly button. After everyone finished, the chanting slowed in tempo and gradually diminished to a unified hum—and then there was silence for a long time. Bev was radiant.

Weeks later, in working out the ramifications of what "I'm me" implied for her in relationships, work, and housing, Bev spoke of the importance to her of her rite of passage, but had as much trouble with specifics as I do now. Jungian vocabulary seems more suited to

* For a discussion of exhibitionism and spontaneity, see Erving Polster and Miriam Polster, *Gestalt Therapy Integrated* (New York: Brunner/Mazel, 1973), pp. 238–239.

this sort of experience than Gestalt. I can only say that for me Bev's rite of passage was tribal, powerful, and beautiful.

However, one woman found the ritual disturbing and left the room as the group began to embellish Bev's stomach. In touch with the tribal feeling, she had a fantasy of a human sacrifice, especially as we were using a red pen. Since the common theme of many rituals is death to one phase or self and rebirth into another, she probably was, in a sense, accurate, but in touch with only half of the experience on a literal, rather then metaphorical, level.

One of the characteristics of the line game is its flexibility. As described, it can be used to focus on one person, yet actively involve other members of the group. It can also be used by the group as a whole. The latter use I have found particularly appropriate at the first of several sessions to get people actively in touch with each other and as a respite of play for a group that has been working on intense material and needs refreshment.*

Most effectively, the leader needs to balance and swing between being unabashedly directive at times and, at others, welcoming suggestions and passing the leadership to others. In an atmosphere of psychological safety and lightness, the leader extends an invitation to play. To allow themselves to play, many adults require that the rules of any particular game include the impossibility of making a mistake. As the episodes of the game unfold and build momentum, I have noticed even cautious people get into the act, apparently having accepted the unthreatening nature of this

* To appreciate the breadth of experiences using art media, see Janie Rhyne, *The Gestalt Art Experience* (Monterey, Calif.: Brooks Cole, 1973).

sort of happening. The following summary of five game episodes illustrates how a group chose to use the invitation to play.

Draw Yourself Out. Teri, the first in the group to play the line game, made her strokes decisively. When I explained that she could direct her own show, she asked if others could draw too. I bowed. She decided that by passing the chalk in relay, people would add to her original lines. Then, with her direction, they enacted a drama of movement and sound based on their contributions to the resulting drawing. Perhaps inevitably, the sounds and positions of each player were marvelously apt for his or her own personality and role in the group.

Strike Your Beat. Prompted by the liveliness, Elizabeth picked up the lead, proposing a game in which the group claps to accompany the rhythm of the dancer, and he chooses the next dancer, who can alter the step and rhythm. Everyone danced in turn, presenting a great variety of tempos and styles.

Song of Sorts. Since people were out of breath by now, I shifted to a sitdown game, mimicking sounds made by group members by drawing a line with chalk as a hieroglyphic for the sound. These ranged from "Om" to a hiccup to the statement "I need more direction." The result was a cross between the Beatles' "Number 9" and a composition by John Cage.

Wild Beasts. Someone thought of being your favorite animal, which was amended to being the opposite of your favorite animal. This led to interesting interactions of which I had an extremely limited view, as I was a sea turtle. In subsequent discussion a person who had been angry about not getting enough attention from the group—the hugging koala bear—complained of being gravely misunderstood as an attacker.

Talking Statue. The group agreed to Milford's proposal to make a human sculpture. She arranged people in positions that expressed her view of their interrelationships and conveyed her own artistic sense of mass and form. She invited us each to say a line. A few were "Who is running this show, anyway?" "Forgive them, Lord," "My balance is precarious!" and the familiar "I need more direction."

My experiences playing nonverbal and verbal games have brought me to two interesting fields for further research and experimentation, one epistemological and one physiological.

The first requires an understanding of Gregory Bateson's analysis of the nature of play and fantasy, which deserves much more generous treatment than the hint possible here. He sees play as a sophisticated communication involving a relationship between primary- and secondary-process thinking.* He points out that, to play, we must have a common frame, or set of limits understood by all parties. Often this frame is not explicit or even conscious (e.g., the adverse reaction to the ritual in Rite of Passage above). One reason for difficulties of communication and relationship is that a person may have different frames from others, different uses of levels of abstraction. Bateson suggests that the process of psychotherapy can be explored in this context as a series of implicit changes in the client's "set of rules for the making and understanding of messages."†

The second field of study vital to further comprehension of what sorts of experiences might be most fruitful for expanded learning is brain physiology and function.

* Gregory Bateson, "A Theory of Play and Fantasy," in his *Steps to an Ecology of Mind* (New York: Ballantine Books, 1972), pp. 177–193.

† *Ibid.*, p. 191.

When we combine nonverbal expressive modes, words used poetically, and words used conceptually, the two hemispheres of our brains are communicating, producing the synthesis of the "we" who experience. It is likely that both nonverbal patterning (including "the set of rules for making and understanding messages") and the activity of play are the province of the nondominant hemisphere of the brain. In "The Other Side of the Brain: An Appositional Mind,"* Joseph Bogan reviews the research on the functions of the hemispheres and clarifies the issues open for further research, which are many. The role of the nondominant hemisphere is still somewhat mysterious. Explorations and descriptions of its function are likely to reveal much more than we now understand about emotional experience, perception of pattern, spatial relationships, music, visual arts, and so on.

Gestalt therapy, among others, has been finding some people "stuck in their heads," using verbal, linear thought patterns to limit their perceptions and contact with themselves, others, and their environment. Perhaps we will modify that phrase to "stuck in their left hemispheres." There may be another, quite different set of consequences if one is "stuck in the right hemisphere." Experiences that put us in touch with both hemispheres and permit integration of perceptual modes seem to be readily available—even by drawing two lines on a sheet of paper.

* In *The Nature of Human Consciousness*, ed. Robert E. Ornstein (San Francisco: W. H. Freeman, 1973), pp. 101–125.

Social Dreamwork and Gestalt Therapy

Joel Latner, Ph.D.

Dreams are a sort of creative process, don't you think? My films come from the same factory.
—Ingmar Bergman

Dreams have always had a special place in psychology. For Freud they were the royal road to the unconscious. For Jung they were messages from the oracle of the developing self. They became Fritz Perls's primary therapeutic focus in his later years. Dreams have had a similar special place in history. They have been chronicled as bearers of prophecy, media of advice and counsel in the courts of kings, and vehicles of self-discovery.

In everyday life the role of dreams is ambiguous. Our culture allots as little opportunity for integrating our dreams into our lives as it allots for integrating most of our other feelings. We have little encouragement to make our dreams part of the currency of our contacts with the objects and people that are important to us.

An earlier version of this essay was published in the Fall 1972 issue of *Voices: The Art and Science of Psychotherapy*. My thanks to the editor for permission to include it in this volume.

Hence we have no way to permit them to transform our reality and our behavior. On the other hand, everyone dreams, spontaneously creating intense and personal stories of grace, beauty, wisdom, and power. Dreaming is the metaphor we most often use in our ordinary language to refer to our aspirations.

Dreaming is not always as anomalous in other cultures as it is in ours, and many so-called primitive peoples have developed methods for working with dreams and fantasies that amplify our own therapies. The Senoi and the Negritos, small tribes who inhabit the Malaysian rain forest, use a psychotherapy that provides a highly effective format for the integration of the dreams of tribal members and their waking lives.*

Briefly, their dreamwork is of two kinds: One consists of understanding dreams by having the dreamer live out his or her identification with his dream creations. This method is quite similar to the dreamwork identified with Gestalt therapy.†

The second part of their dreamwork is specifically concerned with infusing the energy and contents of dreams into the social intercourse of the tribal group.

* The Senoi are known primarily through Kilton Stewart's influential article "Dream Theory in Malaya," in *Altered States of Consciousness: A Book of Readings*, ed. Charles T. Tart (New York: Wiley, 1969). See also Stewart's *Pygmies and Dream Giants* (New York: Norton, 1954; Harper & Row, Harper Colophon Books, 1975) for an account of his anthropological and personal journey in Malaysia. Stewart wrote a number of articles on the Senoi; another is reprinted in *Sources*, ed. Theodore Roszak (New York: Harper & Row, Harper Colophon Books, 1972).

† Good examples of Gestalt dreamwork are to be found in Fritz Perls's *Gestalt Therapy Verbatim* (Lafayette, Calif.: Real People Press, 1969; New York: Bantam, 1971), more than a dozen of his demonstration films, and the recent *Dreams and Nightmares: A Book of Gestalt Therapy Seminars*, ed. Jack Downing and Robert Marmorstein (New York: Harper & Row, 1974).

In contrast to the method described above, where the work is seen primarily (as it is in our therapies) as centering around the individual and the course of his life, this aspect of their dreamwork centers around the interpersonal, on the relationship of the dreamer to his social reality. Dreams are not worked directly—they are not developed, interpreted, explained, made familiar, or acted out. Instead, they are *put to use* in social settings as part of the interactions of the tribal members. The arena for working out a dream is the daily contacts the dreamer has with people he knows, and the benefit that accrues to him is that it alters those contacts. This is social dreamwork.

Using dreams socially might include:

- telling your dreams to people you know—to casual acquaintances and close friends—as you would comment on the weather, what you did last night, or where your head is at
- telling dreams to the friends and acquaintances who appear in them or telling them only that you have dreamed about them
- telling dreams to close friends on a regular basis—for example, at dinner or on commuting trips
- meeting regularly with others in a dream group for the purpose of sharing and working on dreams

In the context of Gestalt therapy, social dreamwork has some special appeals. First, it necessitates that we share the part of ourselves that is expressed by our dreams with others. Like some other aspects of Gestalt practice—doing individual work in a group setting and demonstrating Gestalt work on film and before large audiences, for example—it implies that it is desirable for us to be more public about who we are and how we feel than we are habitually. Not only will no harm come to us, but we will reap an enriched sense of our own expressiveness and of the possibilities for relating to and knowing the world we are a part of. The foundation of this attitude is the Buberian conviction that we discover ourselves in our relationships with others.

The second appeal of social dreamwork in Gestalt therapy relates to the concept of the contact boundary —the meeting place between us and the world of our experience. Fritz Perls distinguished three different arenas of contact: the inner zone, our contact with our inner sensations and perceptions; the middle zone, our contact with our thoughts, opinions, fantasies, and dreams; and the outer zone, our apprehension of what is outside our skins. In terms of psychotherapy and personal growth, social dreamwork is a medium we can use to bring these aspects of our contact together. It engages all three at the same time—inner, middle, and outer. In fact, social dreamwork utilizes our social experience more fully than most other therapeutic activities permit.

In general, people are interested in hearing about dreams. They respond with a lively curiosity. When we tell our dreams to others, they take it as a gift. And, of course, it is. It is sharing a part of the dreamer with the other person. Most often those about whom we dream are touched when we tell them we have dreamed of them. Even when the circumstances portrayed in the dream are not flattering to them, telling friends or colleagues that we have dreamed of them makes an impact on them. Such a gesture is often greeted with "Thank you very much for telling me" or "I feel good that you told me about that dream." So one benefit of these techniques is to foster a simple yet intimate form of interaction. This benefits both parties. For the dreamer an additional benefit is making permeable the division between his private and public selves. He is opening a part of himself to others, showing to others the metaphoric language of his emotions.

Sharing dreams is a relatively painless way of doing this. It evokes little resistance on the part of the dreamer and much respect from the receivers. These benefits come from the use to which dreams are put. They are independent of any meaning that might be attributed to the dreams either by the dreamer or the dream receiver.

Sometimes the content of a dream heightens the contact.

> I dreamt that Gene, a fellow student, was a large white Russian bear, a dancing bear in a circus, tethered to a post, turning in time to the music of a circus band. I told him my dream—it was the second dream I had had of him in two weeks—and he thanked me for telling him. He seemed very touched and thoughtful. Then he added, "You know, I can see something of myself in that dream. I really can."

While the people who figure in our dreams are drawn to our own purposes, their appearance and behavior are usually based on an insight by the dreamer into the person being dreamed about. Characters and objects appear in our dreams because we need a certain emotional quality in our dreams at that time and we have perceived that they have those attributes. Here again, and in contrast to typical Gestalt dreamwork, these procedures speak as much to the reality outside us as to our projections—as much to our outer-zone contact as to our inner- and middle-zone experience.

> I had been aware for several months that remnants of feelings of anger toward my father interfered in my dealings with other people. I had been trying to work them through in the past months. One night I dreamed a bus boy in a cafeteria took the dishes I wasn't finished with from the table where I was eating with friends.

The bus boy was in his forties, a Puerto Rican whom I knew represented my father. I wanted to object, but I was intimidated by his hostility.

I sent the dream to my father, with a note saying I thought he had injured me, and that I thought therefore he owed me a gift. He wrote back a note saying he was furious that I had dreamed he was an angry menial. That angry exchange was one of many we had during that time. They resulted in an alteration of our relationship which brings us a little closer to the one I want with him.

This passage also illustrates another social dreamwork procedure: If you do someone an injury of any kind in a dream, you must give him a gift. The gift should be commensurate in some way with the misdeed. If someone does you an injury, you must tell him, and he is obliged to give you a gift.

This works better in a situation such as a dream group or in a culture like the Senoi, for whom such regulations can be enforced by the culture and handed down in specific cases by shamans, their physician-psychologist-priests. There, all the members of the group are parties to the agreement. In adapting them to our very different social and cultural situation, I have tried to keep to the spirit of these procedures, as can be seen in the reports that follow. The first concerns a woman who had heard me speak enthusiastically about social dreamwork.

Marija approached me today somewhat tremulously and said she thought I owed her a gift. I said, "All right, what happened?" As I said that, I began to think what sort of gift I could get for her. After a while, though, the intensity of her words drove that from my mind.

She said she dreamed she was in half a dozen social settings, one after the other. Each of them had been important parts of her life in the past. In each setting,

I was surrounded by a group of her friends, and I was saying bad things about her.

As I heard her dream, I had a mounting spontaneous impulse to kiss her. (She is an attractive woman nearly twenty years older than I whom I have been on casual terms with.) I held it back till she had finished, and then I kissed her very directly, on the lips. When I stopped, she began to cry. I was very moved, too. It was clear that my kiss was my gift, and it had touched her very deeply. (Later, a friend said I had made up for "bad-mouthing" her by "good-mouthing" her.)

Another adaptation, not involving a dream at all, is described below.

At a student meeting, I found Ted irritating to listen to, even when he wasn't attacking me. I got pissed off at him and challenged him to a fight. He refused. Later, I began to feel he hadn't warranted that kind of anger. Whatever I was angry about, most of it wasn't him. I found a book of mine I thought he would like and I put it in his box. That finished the incident for me, and I haven't thought about it since, until now.

The further the dream subject is from the dreamer, the more difficult it is to entice the former to be part of the dreamwork rules. In the father-related dream cited above, the dream subject would not participate. In the instance that follows, the outcome is different.

I dreamed that Ev, a friend and teacher whom I never got to know as well as I would have liked, was instrumental in having me sacked from an institution where I was working. I got angry at him and he ran away.

I wrote to him and told him my dream, the second I'd had and written to him about in two months. This time I explained about the rules for gift giving. I said I thought I owed him a gift and he owed me one. I wrote that my gift was this letter. One week later, I received a letter from Ev in which he expressed his curiosity and concern about my dreams of him, but said he had not thought of a suitable gift. I felt very good receiving his note—that was a gift!

The dream rules are not artificial. They seem to be codifications of impulses toward furthering personal relations and developing ourselves. Note also that it is not necessary to understand the dream in order to use it. The dream's content is a spur for action, a stimulus for an interaction. In Gestalt terms, these procedures are exercises and experiments, new ways of behaving that provide us with the possibility of discovering something new about ourself.

We speak in Gestalt therapy of keeping the process going. By this we mean that the transformations in ourselves that we call growth occur when we permit ourselves to stay in touch with things as they are, to discover all the relevant aspects of what we are involved in, and to let the energy our contact creates develop according to the situation's requirements and possibilities and our own organismic judgments. This is letting the river run its own course—and at the same time being the river. We cannot *make* things happen without aborting the spontaneous process by which the new invention—the new gestalt—will occur.

While this letting go is a recognition of spontaneity, it is also a disciplined activity requiring our full attention and participation. Keeping the process going means doing what we can to recognize what the present event requires of us and acceding to that, going with it—going with the process. The rules for social dreamwork keep the process of our growth moving by asking that we take some action based on what we have dreamed.

It is not necessary that each of our acts be the best one available in the situation, though that would be most desirable and most efficient. The process is necessarily one of trial and error. What is from one perspective a mistake is from the perspective of the ongoing process simply one more aspect of our exploration and development as we move toward the coming gestalt. Each makes its contribution. I am reminded of the Zen master's question, "Can you tell me the ninety-nine times you miss the bull's-eye have nothing to do with the time you hit it?" It is essential that we continue to experiment and play with what we are in touch with. It is much less important that we always be right. If we keep the energy flowing by staying in touch with ourselves and the rest of the field and if we do what is required, the new transformation will be the best one we can create.

The process by which the dreamer prepares to use his dream may be a therapeutic part of the dreamwork. In one case from a dream group, a group member was obliged to find a gift for another member whom he had offended in a recent dream. After two weeks the dreamer told the group that he was encountering the same kind of problem in making a decision about the gift as he often did in his life—but in an especially clear way.

In the following case, the instructions could not be carried out by the dreamer. Nevertheless, the failure itself was illuminating to her.

> I dreamed my lover was in the back seat of a car. I was driving, making love to a woman I did not know. I was very upset and spoke to someone about it, who said I ought to tell John my dream and ask him to recompense me. I said I couldn't do that, because I thought it was too much to ask.

Perhaps the most familiar example of using dreams in our culture is the dream that is understood and responded to as a command. In such a case, the rule is: If you know what a dream is telling you to do, do it.

> I have been a student of Zen for nearly four years. Since coming here I have thought about going to the local center, but have preferred to sit zazen alone. This week I had the third of a series of dreams in which I am instructed to go to the Zen Center. I dreamt an attractive Oriental woman whom I have dreamt about before is suggesting I go to the Zen Center. I say I'm not sure I want to go, and she says she will go with me if I prefer.
>
> I realized I had better go, and I did, last Saturday, but the center did not seem to be what I wanted, so I have not returned; nor have I dreamt about it since.

Notice here that this dream keeps the process going; it doesn't find the right answer. It says only, "Try this; this is what is to be done next."

The Senoi treat dreams in which a person or object is seen in a favorable light with a rule: If someone or something is kind to you in a dream, treat them as a special friend and seek out their company. If, for example, the dreamer dreams that someone is helpful to him, he should befriend that person. If he dreams of making love to someone, he should court her, if he can. If he cannot, if the other person is married or the relationship would be incestuous and prohibited by tribal law, the dreamer is instructed to dream the dream again and rip off the mask of his lover in order to find out what other person or demon is using her face. Again, we can see how this promotes the interpersonal process.

The Senoi are taught to be able to redream their dreams according to instructions given to dreamers by shamans. Often these instructions require that the dreamer continue with the activity of the dream until its conclusion, and its conclusion must contain a socially useful product. A Senoi may be instructed not to leave a dream lover until he or she has taught the dreamer a song he can bring back to his waking life and teach the others.

Unlike the Senoi, we don't learn at an early age to redream our dreams and direct their activities. I and others I know of who have been adapting Senoi practices to our culture have had scant success with instructed dreaming. An alternative, commonly used in Gestalt therapy, is waking fantasy, in which the dreamer is asked to relax and close his or her eyes and to dream the dream while awake. In this way it is possible to be in touch with the dream process without sleeping. Using this technique, the dreamer can be asked to continue his dream or he can be asked to alter it.

This example of Gestalt dreamwork illustrates its similarity to the Senoi process of instructed redreaming.

> I dreamed I was on a sandy, sunny beach. I walked up some wooden stairs to a beach house on a sandy cliff overlooking a beach. Albert Einstein was inside, at a desk filled with books and papers. I was asked to continue the dream, and I did this by conversing with Einstein about my future, my work, and my relations with women. He functioned as a wise old part of me, and I felt clear and relieved when I was finished.

This second example contains an alteration of the dream process, as a result of an intervention by the therapist.

> I dreamed I was at the top of the tallest building in the city. I wanted to go down. I went down, very afraid the whole time, on a tightrope that stretched from the tower to a major intersection far below. When I got to the street, I was a pinwheel man, walking mechanically, with sparks but no life. Tom had me reexperience the dream until the point where I was atop the tower; then he asked me to see if I could fly. I did, and I could. I wasn't afraid, and I reveled in my newfound freedom of movement.

In form, this instruction is identical to what Stewart reports of Senoi shamans. I have encouraged students and clients engaged in social dreamwork to see if they can turn their dreams to the kind of creative purposes the Senoi regularly do. And again, while it isn't a regular occurrence, people have been able to direct dream material into artistic forms—plots for short stories, images for poetry and paintings, situations for songs, musical phrases. Others have been able to use creatively the waking fantasy skill that dreamwork utilizes.

Drawing our originality out of this part of ourselves is not limited to this kind of dreamwork, though I suspect it enhances its success. The most familiar example to me is Kikule, the Nobel Prize winning chemist who sought without success to understand the molecular structure of benzene. Eventually the answer came in a dream, in the form of a snake with its tail in its mouth, showing the way in which the benzene ring is formed into a circle, with the end of the chain being also its beginning. I believe most creative enterprises draw on this capacity of ours in some fashion.

When ought a dream to be used according to the procedures I have described, and when ought a dream to be worked? I know of no formula. Individual work, such as that regularly done in Gestalt therapy, is useful with most dreams, to flesh out their full import. On the other hand, some dreams lend themselves to being worked and others to being used. The emotional tone and content of the dream tell you what to do with it. Dreams that need to be worked arouse curiosity and have a quality of being interrupted, unfinished, or enigmatic. Dreams that might be fruitfully used often impel to action a dreamer familiar with the techniques discussed above. In general, the personality of the dreamer and the nature of the issues he is dealing with in his life are the most important factors determining whether dreams get used or worked. A good rule of thumb is: If you can think of a use to put a dream to, try it out. Remember, too, that it isn't necessary to choose one alternative to the exclusion of the other.

One kind of dream stands midway between using and working dreams. The following is an example.

> I am sitting on a bench in the park. A man comes by, and I know he is coming for me. He looks at me and then wordlessly walks on. I notice that he has looked at the top of my head, and I become aware that I am wearing a shower cap. I realize that I am hiding my hair under my shower cap, and I understand I am hiding my femininity.
>
> I wake up knowing that the dream is a statement about me: I mask my femininity.

A dream of this kind is about the kind of person the dreamer is at that time in his life. It is an existential statement about the dreamer. It could be worked, and it certainly suggests behavioral changes to the dreamer; but dreams of this sort, when accompanied by the kind of understanding this dreamer voices, seem to be a synthesis by the self of an important aspect of the dreamer's life. In dreams like the one above, the message may be familiar to the dreamer or it may be the kind of surprise that is immediately known to be an accurate reflection of the dreamer's existence. These statements may reformulate something we know or make us aware of something we are ready to know. At times, as in the following dream, it seems that the purpose of this kind of dream is to provide support rather than knowledge.

> I am in a small audience room. I know it is at the Vatican, though the room is off a library area where I used to study. Pope John is there, simply dressed, and younger in years than when he was a pope. He speaks English as though it were his native tongue, in a strong and warm voice.

> Though I am not a Catholic, he is a spiritual teacher, and I am there to tell him the course of my life. I do this, and I say that I have struggled to be what I am now.
>
> I say it has been painful for me.
>
> He listens sympathetically and touches me on my shoulder. He says I am doing well and I should press onward. He says he knows it is difficult, but I should persevere. As I hear him acknowledge the difficulty I have experienced, I cry. I wake feeling very good.

Here the dream experience affirms the course that the dreamer's life is taking, offering solace, comfort, and approval.

There are two aspects of the self that are not normally a part of our consciousness. One is our unfinished business, the events and experiences of our life that we have not worked through and left behind. The other is our potential, the momentum of our becoming what we are capable of. These are intimately related facets of the same urge toward maturity, for unfinished business cannot exist unless the organism needs to grow and is not able to. The notion of unfinished business, like any notion of our dis-ease, depends on acknowledging that there is something basic and essential in each of us, and that our lives are defined by our attempts to realize it. Notwithstanding our pliable, adaptive aspects, we have a grain, and things we do and things that are done to us go with or against our grain. From this perspective growth is moving toward our identification with all of our essential nature.

This part of us can speak to us, as in the last dream. It speaks through our dreams if we listen and try to understand, and if we respond to them. Working our dreams into our waking lives, we stay close to the possibilities of our growth.

Unmasking the Face and Facing the Mask: A Gestalt Approach to Facial Therapy

Jack L. Rosenberg, Ph.D., D.D.S.

There is probably not one of us who has practiced psychotherapy who has not sat opposite someone, poignantly aware of the deepest of human emotions pervading the person's presence, yet noticing that his face appears contained, masklike, and e-motionless—desperately holding back the depth of sadness or terror, anger, fear, rage, or other feelings by controlling his expression, "saving," as it were, his "face," preventing the expression of his inner feelings. The frustration for us as therapists is that we know, through our own experience, that the expressing and the experiencing of those emotions will lift the cloud of despair and free the energy of life for which they so desperately long.

One problem as I see it is that psychotherapists ignore the face as a gateway to affect. The face, after all, is the major means of expressing emotions as well as for hiding them; yet even though this is common knowledge, it is rarely focused upon as a primary source of, or at least a most vulnerable opening to, the inner self or being.

Rainer Maria Rilke captured the feeling that I have so often experienced in my work with facial therapy, the feeling that my clients have of being unmasked and naked—vulnerable, yes, but also cleared of many of the "masking" emotions that take months or years to pass.

> . . . I have never been aware before how many faces there are. There are quantities of human beings, but there are many more faces, for each person has several. There are people who wear the same face for years; naturally it wears out, it gets dirty, it splits at the folds, it stretches like gloves one has worn on a journey. These are thrifty, simple people; they do not change their face, they never even have it cleaned. It is good enough, they say, and who can prove to them the contrary? The question, of course, arises, since they have several faces, what do they do with the others? But sometimes, too, it happens that their dogs go out with them on. And why not? A face is a face.
>
> Other people put their faces on, one after the other, with uncanny rapidity, and wear them out. At first it seems to them they are provided for always; but they scarcely reach forty—and they have come to the last. This naturally has something tragic. They are not accustomed to taking care of faces, their last is worn through in a week, has holes, and in many places is thin as paper; and then little by little the under layer, the no-face, comes through, and they go about with that.
>
> But the woman, the woman; she had completely collapsed into herself, forward into her hands. It was at the corner of Rue Notre-Dame-des-Champs. I began to walk softly as soon as I saw her. When poor people are reflecting they should not be disturbed. Perhaps their idea will yet occur to them.
>
> The street was too empty; its emptiness was bored; it caught my step from under my feet and clattered about with it hither and yon, as with a wooden clog. The woman was startled and pulled away too quickly out of herself, too violently, so that her face remained

> in her two hands. I could see it lying in them, its hollow form. It cost me indescribable effort to stay with those hands and not to look at what had torn itself out of them. I shuddered to see a face from the inside, but still I was much more afraid of the naked flayed head without a face.*

I first began my work with facial expressions not as a psychotherapist but by concentrating on facial aesthetics as a dentist. I had been practicing restorative dentistry for a number of years. My attention was aimed at making people look better by replacing broken teeth or repairing disfigured and discolored teeth with prosthetic appliances or jackets (caps), and so forth, as well as resupporting the facial tissue and musculature that had begun to sag because of lost teeth or the loss of bony structure surrounding the teeth due to accidents, aging, or infection.

As I did this kind of dentistry I was continually struck with the persistence of muscular habits (fixed muscular patterns) that remained even after the origin of the habit, the structural defect, was removed. For instance, a woman with a disfigured and discolored front tooth had a habit of pulling her lips over her front teeth when she smiled. The expression was used to cover her tooth so that no one could see it when she smiled. After I restored her tooth to its natural shape and color, she continued to have the covering habit—much to my frustration.

At that time, I was being introduced to the work of Ida Rolf (structural integration), so I began "Rolfing"—using deep massage of the face—out of my frustration at trying to alter muscular habits or fixed muscular patterns that were so rigidly held even after the need for them was changed. Much to my surprise, it worked!

What I found was that, although I could alter the

* Rainer Maria Rilke, *The Notebooks of Malta Laurids Brigge.*

facial muscular pattern very dramatically through massage, after a while the expression would return. It was as though I could change the muscle, but the face itself had a masklike pattern that would return again to its original "character" (although it took me a while to discover the return of the muscular habit). It was during this period of treating faces with massage that I became very enthusiastic about my results, and I began to teach facial massage in some of my groups. I was certain that I had discovered the means to a nonsurgical face lift by developing an intricate and complicated way to release the muscular patterns of the face with massage.

I remember one incident in particular. I was teaching my massage technique to a group of residents at Esalen. We had been working for some time when one of the subjects receiving the massage began to cry and started into a very frightening (for him) reaction that centered about the feeling of being suffocated. As we worked with this terrifying emotion by Gestalt means, it became evident that he had regressed to a very early age—approximately six or seven—when general anesthesia had been forced upon him for a broken nose. All the fear and terror that had been there during those early years were again being expressed in the "here and now"—completely, and in a very real way.

After a number of similar incidents, my interest shifted from the face as the object of investigation to the emotion or affect released by massage. This seemed to me to be a reasonable means through which to contact the deeper emotions. Even though my interest was in the affect, when I finally developed my total facial technique, the final results were a changing of the total facial quality, a reowning of lost parts of the face for the client—both in the ability to express and in the flexibility of the fixed muscular pattern.

Still, the most profound effect of the massage was the strength of emotions and the depth from which they were released during massage. The problem was somehow to integrate the release of the emotion with the facial expression in the "here and now." For this, my video feedback method has proved most valuable.

Although I cannot predict the exact emotion that will be released by massage of any particular area of the face, because that is very difficult to do, I have been able to chart some of the more pertinent areas of the face and the emotions I have observed as most often being associated with these areas. (See Figure 2 and Table 1, pages 152–153.)

It may be useful to present some of the assumptions and theoretical background for these techniques. They are based on Gestalt therapy concepts, the Reichian concept of the muscular nature of repression, and recent evidence from neurophysiology. In Gestalt therapy, as developed by Fritz Perls, one way to look at neurosis is as a manifestation of "holes" in the personality caused by a failure to complete gestalts.

Living is a process of constant formation and completion of gestalts that leads to a constantly shifting awareness. When the completion of an important gestalt is blocked, it then becomes a "hole" in the personality that must be filled if growth is to continue. One technique used in Gestalt therapy, then, is to establish a continuum of awareness—that is, a state of being in the present, in the here-and-now—in which the patient reports his perceptions of what he is experiencing. In doing this the patient and therapist can more immediately recognize any interruption in the process of awareness. These interruptions of sensing or reporting are believed by Perls to represent the emergence of unfinished emotional situations. The patient will avoid this emerging feeling or completion of a gestalt in a *phobic* manner—that is, a flight into fantasy, rehearsing, anxiety expression, and so on. Thus the therapist has a clue to the emotionally charged area the patient is avoiding. He can then proceed to bring the unfinished situation to awareness so that it can be dealt with.

As a Gestalt therapist I work as a catalyst by providing a situation in which a person can experience his avoidance—his "being stuck," his impasse—and then by frustrating the avoidance still further until the client is willing to mobilize his own resources to pass through the "stuck area," or impasse. The blocking, or avoidance, is expressed in movements of the whole body, as well as in facial expression and voice. *The therapeutic goal is to integrate awareness and attention—a deliberate way of "listening" to the emerging foreground figure.* This brings emotions to consciousness by centering the awareness on the patient himself, specifically his facial expression. (I shall explain this more fully when I discuss the video technique.)

Wilhelm Reich, in his character-analytic work,* spoke of "armoring" in the form of fixed muscular attitudes. His formulation of a muscular theory of repression speaks more clearly of the chronic automatically functioning mode of reaction that he called "character armoring." Reich states:

> It is as if the affective personality put on an armor, a rigid shell on which the knocks from the outer world as well as the inner demand rebound. This armor makes the individual less sensitive to unpleasure but it also reduces his libidinal and aggressive mobility and, with that, his capacity for pleasure and achievement.

This is most evident in the muscles of expression of the face.

* Wilhelm Reich, *Character Analysis* (New York: Farrar, Straus & Giroux, 1968).

Ida Rolf has contributed to the development of direct muscle stimulation in her work on structural integration, in which she states: "In any attempt to create an integrated individual, an obvious starting place is his physical body."* Her work consists of alteration of the physique by deep massage and changing the fascial layers of musculature; thus, she works with a person's "character" directly. Gellhorn has offered experimental data to substantiate the previous approaches, with particular emphasis on facial expression.

> Proprioceptive discharges contribute to the physiological processes underlying the emotions in two ways: (a) by the setting of the hypothalamic balance which, other conditions being equal, is determined by the posture of the body through the total quantity of proprioceptive impulses impinging on the posterior hypothalamus per unit of time; (b) through facial contraction patterns which lead to afferent discharge via the hypothalamic-cortical system and interact with cutaneous facial impulses of the cortex.

Thus, "It is pointed out that states of abnormal emotional tension are alleviated in various 'relaxation' therapies."†

Tomkins views the face as a primary organ of affect, just as the hand and the fingers are the primary organ of manipulation and exploration.‡ The primacy of both hands and face rests on their very high density of receptor-effector units, whereas the visual and auditory systems are distinguished by a high density of receptor cells and the face (and to a lesser extent the hand) is

* Ida P. Rolf, "Structural Integration," mimeographed (New York: Ida P. Rolf, 1963).

† E. Gellhorn, "Physiological Processes related to Consciousness and Perception," *Brain* 77 (1954): 401–415.

‡ Silvan S. Tomkins, *Affect, Imagery, Consciousness,* vol. 1, *The Positive Affects* (New York: Springer, 1962).

also engaged in extremely heavy two-way traffic communication. Whatever it sends via tongue and facial muscles, it also receives as feedback. For example, changes in blood flow to the face, which produce changes in the temperature of the face, are also received as feedback, most notably in blushing. Tomkins emphasizes the four following facts to support his view of the face as a primary organ of affect (and, in relation to my massage technique, therefore the most obvious area for direct stimulation):

1. The greater density and early development of receptor-effector units in the face
2. The dominance of the face in tactual experiments on children
3. The lesser habituation to startle of the muscles of the face than that of other muscles
4. The absence of fascia in facial muscles, which makes it possible to contract small bundles of these muscles through the extensive branches of the facial nerves and thereby increases the variety of contraction patterns

The face, particularly the mouth, is viewed as a microcosm of the body in the field of oral pathology and dentistry* and reflects the total body health, just as it can express a total body affect. This assumption can be extended to the premise of this paper. Based on this knowledge, with the support of work by Tomkins, Gellhorn, and others, it is possible to understand more clearly why facial expression is useful in releasing blocked or repressed emotion.

A more complete understanding can be made by again drawing from Gestalt theory. Just as Perls detected "holes" in a person's perception of himself, it

* Nathan A. Shore, *Occlusal Equilibration and Temporomandibular Joint Dysfunction* (Philadelphia: Lippincott, 1959).

follows that there can also be "holes" in one's perception of one's face when viewing immediate video feedback. These "avoided" or "unnoticed" areas, when brought to awareness, become mobile; and the emotion or incomplete gestalt associated with these blocked areas comes to awareness, to be integrated into the person's total functioning. Awareness of blocked expression of emotion is prompted by the use of direct massage or stimulation. These theoretical bases will become clearer as I detail the process I have developed in facial therapy.

TECHNIQUES FOR USE OF IMMEDIATE VIDEO FEEDBACK

The use of immediate video feedback technique is not an innovation in psychotherapy. My suggested method of use does differ in the manner in which the video is used from that reported in previous accounts. The major difference is in the physical arrangement of the room and the role of the TV monitor in relation to the patient.

The equipment I use consists of four chairs, one adjustable table, the videotape recording system, and two TV, or video, monitors. (See Figure 1.) One monitor—the major monitor—is placed on a vertically adjustable table. Three chairs are placed in front of it, and the video camera is mounted directly over it. The second video monitor is placed behind the subject directly in the therapist's view, so that he can see what the subject is seeing in the major monitor and still look at the subject directly. In order that the consistency of what is seen by the subject can be controlled, he is seated in chair I and the video camera is adjusted to such a height and distance that his face covers the

FIGURE 1

PLACEMENT OF SUBJECT, THERAPIST, AND EQUIPMENT IN IMMEDIATE VIDEO FEEDBACK TECHNIQUE

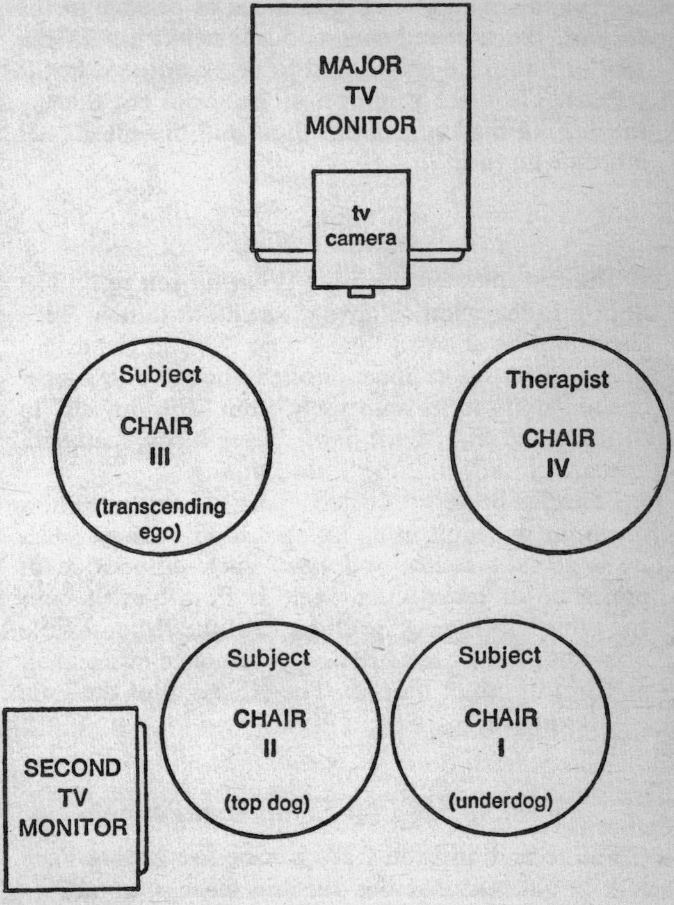

monitor screen with little or no background showing.

As the session begins, the subject is seated in chair I; the therapist is seated in his chair; the video monitor is projecting the patient's own image. The therapy involves utilizing each of the chair positions as aspects of the subject's attitude and encouraging direct encounter with the videotape image in each position. The flow of the therapy is kept as much as possible in the present, the here-and-now, and any references to the past or future are encouraged to be experienced in the present. There are a number of directions the therapy can take. I shall summarize these and present a brief rationale for each.

What Do You See?

The first question I ask is "What do you see?" The answer to this question gives me a clue as to how much the subject is oriented to the objective and the extent of his subjective or inner-directed energy. The answer to the inquiry varies immensely, from "I see myself" to "I see a TV set," "I see hair," "I see a boy, man, girl, woman, chick," etc., to "I see nothing."

I have, in other words, gathered some clue as to how much the patient is using his optical power, how much he is actually seeing, and how much dissociation or projection or retroflection there is from himself onto the subject he is viewing. One end of the response scale would be "I don't see anything"—complete dissociation and lack of use of his eyes. The other end of the scale is "I see myself."

How Do You Feel about That Person?

The second question I ask is aimed at getting some sort of evaluation of the self and feelings, as well as encouraging feelings. Thus I ask, "How do you feel about that person on the screen?" Again the range is very large—"I don't like her," "I like what I see, "I like me," "I like her or him," etc. I tend to follow the negative response (retroflection); therefore, if the answer is negative, I follow the self-"defacing" tendency by further asking, "What do you not like about her or him?"

The answer to this question is usually a feeling state that is undifferentiated—for example, "I don't like the way she thinks," "She's mean," "She's sad, depressed, worthless, no good, afraid," etc. I try to get that feeling of rejection of the self-projection onto the image by identifying it with the TV image.

Where Do You See That Feeling?

I ask, "Where do you see that feeling?" The subject then projects a feeling onto his or her own image. "I see it in her eyes, mouth," etc. I encourage specific areas for their projection. I now have the patient's self-evaluation or devaluation projected onto his own image.

The next step is to begin to enlarge on the areas that the subject can see. I ask the subject to describe the rest of what he sees. Again I note whether the patient gives an opinion or a description. If the answer is an opinion, I reinforce the identification of the feeling or thought with the specific area of the face—for example, "I see a fat, ugly nose," or "I see messy hair." I also try to begin to separate description from opinion by my repetition and clarification, such as "You *see* your nose and you *think* it's fat and ugly." "You *see* your hair and you *think* it's a mess"—"Where do you see the sadness, joy, stupidity?" etc.

I continue to get a description of what the patient

sees until he stops or runs out of observations, each time differentiating observation from opinion and identifying locations on the screen image. Usually there will be one or more areas of the face that each of us is absolutely unable to see. (In my experience these areas are almost always associated with fixed muscular patterning.) I mentally note this area for reference in the facial massage and also for an unknown area that can be contrasted to a more alive area.

Other clues I note to detect fixed muscular patterning are texture of the skin, puffiness in the area (if present, this may indicate possible edema), and lack of use of tissue and musculature. A thickened and tough skin may be a reaction to loss of feeling in that area (surface anesthesia); sagging indicates loss of collagen and/or atrophy of underlying supporting musculature, as well as which muscles are not being used. The *tone* of the skin is another indication of general health and vitality; yet tightly contracted underlying muscles make the skin lighter in color. Oiliness or dryness is also an indicator of fixed musculature patterning, in that tissue that is mobile and healthy contains a minimum of either.

I also note the direction of lines. This shows where contractions take place and the muscle patterns of movement. Lines are usually along an area of movement, in contrast to the area of fixed muscular patterning. The temperature of the face can be felt by placing the back of the hand approximately one to one and a half inches away from the face. To avoid reaction to the stimulus and loss of objectivity about what is being presented, care should be taken not to touch the subject. I note the temperature differences from area to area in the face and compare different areas. Chronic muscular tension is noted by a decrease in temperature because of the asemia due to muscular contraction. I usually do not check the temperature of a face unless I am going to do a facial massage.

I also look for scars and injuries, nerve loss, or asymmetry. I compare the top of the face with the bottom and each side with the other. This again offers a possible direction in the therapeutic work—for example, the development of an encounter between sides, one that has a scar and one that does not.

The original survey can be facilitated if the face is divided into four bands, or areas. Thus a diagnostic grid can be imposed on the face. (See Figure 2.) These bands must be seen as encircling the head; for example, tension area I–A, B, C, is related to the frontalis and occipitalis and the deep muscles in the base of the skull at the back of the head.

During this portion of the viewing I have the option of working with any of the statements or continuing to the end of the observations of the face on camera. The decision to influence the interview in any particular direction is in many ways intuitively decided, but I can offer some possible explanation for some directions.

Self-Massage

If the area of the face first associated with the feeling is obvious (for instance, "I see sadness." "Where do you see sadness?" "In my eyes and below them"), I may have the subject place his hands, fingers, or palms in that area and massage it. I can then deal with feelings that may be released by the subject's massaging of himself.

Finding areas on which to focus encourages the process of taking sides, then encountering the split or opposing side is more possible. This is beneficial in developing a dialogue with the two voices in the Gestalt top-dog–underdog manner.

FIGURE 2

BANDS I, II, III, IV
AND SAGITTAL SECTIONS A, B, C

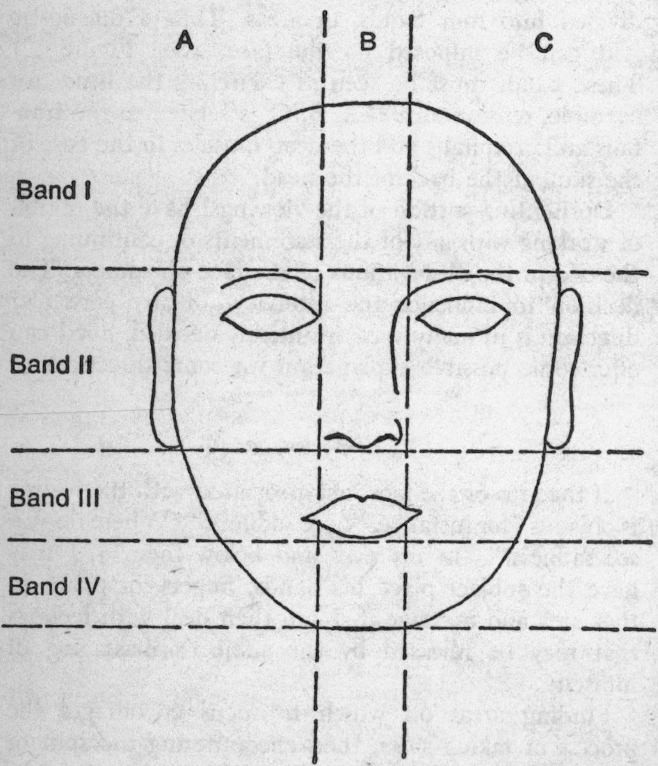

TABLE 1

SUMMARY OF BANDS AND ASSOCIATED AFFECT

Band	Associated affect
Band I	1. Feelings of suffocation, early association with anesthesia
	2. Feelings of wonder or questioning
	3. Fixed look of inquiry
	4. Worry, fretting (associated with corrugator supercilii), "What will I do now?" look
	5. Anger or aggression (particularly associated with temporalis)
	6. Depression, despair (associated with corrugator supercilii and procerus)
Band II	1. Feelings of inadequacy, shame, shyness
	2. Terror (associated with infraorbital foramen)
	3. Tears, free-floating sadness (associated with infraorbital area)
	4. Pleasant feelings associated with laughing
	5. Perception of different odors
Band III	1. Aggression (related to masseter)
	2. Sucking feelings that were prevented
	3. Dependency: "Help me" or "I'm helpless"
	4. Sexual feelings related to oral sex play
	5. Desire to open mouth (external pterygoid), talking
	6. Crying, associated with fear, sorrow
	7. Gagging, expulsion of something (not associated with gag reflex)
Band IV	1. Sucking expression
	2. Pitifulness (particularly associated with mentalis)
	3. Negative feelings, dismissal, "So now what?"
	4. Worry, doubt
	5. Tears

Spontaneous Hand-Face Gestures

I pay very close attention to the hand-face gestures that are made during the observation of the face. These are some of the most powerful clues I work with to develop a split in attitude. For example, "What is your hand saying to your forehead?" In this relationship of hand to face, the body message is one of the most powerful and effective ways of getting to areas of affect. Noting differences in attitude from one area of the face to another can also be useful in developing a split and in the ensuing dialogue; for instance, "I like my eyes but I don't like my chin," or "My left eye is happy and my right eye is sad." Sometimes I have a subject cover one part of his face with a piece of paper to facilitate the taking of sides. A split of feeling may follow any of the twelve quadrants in Figure 2, but it is usually more productive if the splits are spacially further apart—for instance, left-right or top-bottom.

Recall and Recognition of Similarities

I place particular attention on any references to similarity of looks to someone else's—for example, "I have eyes like my father, brother, husband, mother," etc. "My mother used to be just that way, gesture that way, use that expression," etc. I work with these clues immediately by asking the subject to put his father, mother, etc., in chair III (see Figure 1) and tell him or her what is going on at this time. I watch for any clue to a regressive attitude or feeling state. If I suspect that this is happening, I may ask how old the patient feels; then I have him be that age and talk to the father or whoever has similarity that they have observed and developed.

Developing and Observing Ego

The video camera is placed in a manner that does not allow the subject to look himself directly in the eye. This provokes many comments that are useful for beginning to develop the observing-ego function. I may proceed in this way: "Yes, it is impossible to see yourself directly, but then this way it is almost as if you were watching someone else, like a television show. Try to see if you can develop that attitude of observing a TV show. The difference is that you know the character on the screen very well." (At this point, it is also useful to refer to the difference between the way one appears in a mirror and the way one appears on a TV screen.)

I now ask the patient to tell me about that person on the screen or to make up a play or story about that person. As the patient describes himself, he again interjects values or feelings about himself. I can now begin to develop the attitudes in his description. For example: "He is a sad boy who isn't willing to grow up. On the other hand, he has a lot of problems with which to deal and he is trying."

To develop the different themes, I have the subject sit in chair II and act judgmental (enacting the superego function—top dog) and criticize the person on the screen, then move back to chair I and give the other side of the picture (underdog). I develop these attitudes by being aware of posture, voice, and gesture, as well as how the subject looks on the monitor.

There is now an option to develop a conversation between the two attitudes about the person on the screen, or each can continue to talk to that third image on the TV.

Resistance

If I encounter resistance at any point, but particularly at this point, I have the subject move to chair III and describe what is happening and how the characters in chairs I and II are behaving. (In chair III the TV monitor can no longer be viewed; thus, in a sense, the subject becomes the person on the monitor.)

A conversation with either of chairs I or II can be developed; more important, the subject is now facing me directly, and we can work on our relationship or the resistance of "those other two" in chairs I and II.

Another possible tack is to merely play back the videotape of a particular sequence and deal with it as a TV show. I can criticize what is going on or I can defend someone; I can have the subject view a sequence from chair I or chair II; a number of possibilities are now available.

Replaying a sequence is often a very powerful experience and is in itself stimulus enough to contact, affect, and/or arouse regressive feelings.

Once the resistance has been worked through, I have the option of continuing with a verbal approach or starting on a form of facial massage. If I do the facial massage, I utilize the information I have noted from the subject's movement and my observation on the monitor of fixed muscular patterning, along with the other clues I have mentioned. I also keep in mind those areas of his face that he does not see. I never cease to be surprised that, almost universally, there seem to be certain areas of our face that we just cannot see. It is as if, just as there are "holes" in our personality, there are holes in our face that we cannot observe. These "holes," or unobservable areas, are almost always associated with a fixed muscular patterning. In other words, all of us have areas of our face of which we are not aware, areas that we expressed yet have no control over, that we do not "own."*

When the patient returns to the TV monitor after the massage, I ask him to sit for a moment and close his eyes (I do not want him to contaminate his feelings at this time by seeing the video image) and tell me about his experience or feelings during the massage. The massage has usually stimulated some fantasy and/or regressive feelings. I again have the option of dealing with those fantasies or continuing with the therapy by viewing the monitor. If I return to the TV, I repeat the original question, "Tell me what you see?" Universally, there is a difference in what the subject can see after the facial massage (again offering a split to work with—before and after). I can now continue the session until I feel that the subject has reached an impasse, or an area of "stuckness," from which he cannot see a way out, or until I feel he at least has a clear picture of both sides of the conflict as demonstrated in chairs I and II.

Regression to a Specific Age

Often the emotion that is brought out or stimulated by the massage is expressed by crying. This crying may not seem appropriate to what is going on at the time, and I may sense that a child is crying. If this happens, I sometimes ask the patient, "How old are you?" If the answer is "Forty-nine," I may say, "Yes, but how old do you feel?" The answer is now usually an earlier age. I then have the subject play that earlier age and

* For further information and as a guide to facial massage, I refer you to my book *Total Orgasm* (Berkeley, Calif.: Bookworks, 1973), which has a fairly complete description of facial massage and, more importantly, its sequence.

tell me how he feels. He may not be able to complete a sentence or a number of sentences, but he can utter a short sentence or statement like "I can't do it," "Help me," or "Leave me alone." There are a number of these short feeling-state sentences. I then ask, "To whom do you feel you are talking?" or "Who do you want to say this to?" I then can start the process again of taking sides and encountering.

Finding Unfinished Situations

The information connected with the emergence of feelings usually comes from an unfinished situation or series of events in the past. I try to allow and help the patient to finish the situation now. Frequently, in trying to finish an unfinished situation, it is obvious that the patient is holding on to something in the relationship. This becomes evident when you notice the muscles of mastication, the trapezius and the posterior neck. The clue may come as a stiffness or a moving of the jaw, or the stretching of the head or jaw and neck muscles, particularly the temporalis and the masseter. To increase the awareness of the holding-on feeling and also to emphasize the feeling of relief when he lets go, I have the patient hold a folded towel in his posterior teeth. I then put the other end of the towel in my teeth and, keeping eye contact so that the patient stays aware of the "now," I have him pull against me. This experience is very tiring to the muscles of the jaw (muscles of mastication) and the muscles of the posterior of the neck. When the patient seems to be tiring, I have him let go and experience the relief. This usually facilitates the letting-go process.

The process of holding on is usually associated with resentment. I may have a person take the towel and choke it (implosive-type anger) and/or bite on it at the same time, thus allowing the expression of oral as well as manual aggression.

If the patient has a tongue-thrusting or a reverse swallowing pattern, there is a chance that some trauma in relation to a sucking pattern was probably experienced. Thus, during the massage and/or regression, I may encourage the patient to suck the finger or area he used to suck. This is extremely productive in reaching affect.

Stopping the Tape

A gesture or an expression can often be caught on the TV by stopping the tape so that the subject can see the expression in a frozen image. This is a very powerful experience. The feeling that the subject has been avoiding can all of a sudden be shown for a length of time and really be experienced as "out there."

I remember working with a lovely young woman who was continuously giving herself a hard time. I had just paid her a compliment, and she responded in her usual way by verbally pushing me away and not letting in the supporting comment. When we stopped the tape for her to look at it, she could see the anger with which she was rebuffing support. On seeing her expression she said, "That looks like someone who is killing someone else." And it was; in a sense, she was killing herself by not taking in nurture.

The Transition from Observing Ego to Transcending Ego

A subtle difference may take place at this time. Some subjects are able to see objectively and clearly both sides of their internal conflict. This seeing is experienced as objective and clear but still as a problem that they have to deal with. This view is made by what I term an *observing ego*. Others see their internal conflict and struggle quite clearly, as in the observing ego, but are able to carry this a step further and see the problem as a part of an even larger picture of the self. Their insight transcends the earthly struggle to a much more spiritual level. They can then identify a state of being we all share: in Jungian terms, they grasp and identify the depth of the collective unconscious; in spiritual terms, they grasp the cosmic consciousness.

This insight, or shift from observing ego by transcending ego, is always profound and deeply moving for the subject as well as for the therapist. I have found that it is not possible to *make* the experience of transcendence come. It is given by a power not in my control. What I do to facilitate this feeling is to give the following instructions.

I ask the subject to sit in chair III, close his eyes and imagine himself as a one-thousand-year-old person who is very wise and has been on this earth for many years and has seen this conflict happen before and will see the same thing again and again. He can do nothing about the conflict, nor does he care, for it is just the way things are. After each sentence he is to use the words "and that's all right," giving permission for the feelings and the impasse.

If at any time the observing ego or the transcending ego becomes contaminated by judgment, I have the patient move to the chair from which the feeling is more appropriate—that is, the chair of the superego. The observing ego function should be kept uncontaminated by judgments or defensiveness. The voice of the observing ego is positive and yet not involved; that is, from this position the patient can see what is going on and, possibly, can see the solution to the problem without a judgmental approach. It is at this time that the third, or transcending, voice will touch the depths of existence, or religiously speaking, the "soul," of a person. Thus one may transcend the dimensions of everyday conflict to a deeper, more "important" question of existence and being, or of dying. This transition to the third voice and a deeper level is closely related to the process of individuation or self-actualization. The transcending state may not take place, but even if it does not, both aspects of the split will be clearly defined and permission to be that way granted. This in itself removes a pressure and seems to allow for change when the impasse has been described by the observing ego.

Facial therapy is very dramatic, and the depth of the work is universally profound. For this reason, I recommend that the work done with these techniques be used as part of an *ongoing* process in an *ongoing* relationship, and not used in a one-time interview technique. Much of the material stimulated in the interview will come up again and again, and will need to be worked through. If used in a one-time process, material may come up that is too overwhelming for the subject to understand, and thus he may block himself from hearing it again for some time.